RIVER *of* GOLD

NARRATIVES AND EXPLORATION OF THE GREAT LIMPOPO

D1613041

PETER NORTON   MICHAEL GARDNER   CLIVE WALKER

JACANA

First published by Jacana Media
(Pty) Ltd in 2015

10 Orange Street
Sunnyside, Auckland Park 2092
South Africa
+2711 628 3200
www.jacana.co.za

Design by Shawn Paikin,
Set in Goudy Old Style 10.5/15pt
Printed and bound in Malaysia by
Times Offset (M) Sdn. Bhd.
Job no. 002598

ISBN 978-1-4314-2338-5

See a complete list of Jacana titles at
www.jacana.co.za

PREVIOUS SPREAD: Magnificent trees of many descriptions abound alongside the banks of the
Shashe River, which millions of years ago carried the bulk of the water from the interior of Botswana.

COVER: Golden light plays across the great Limpopo from the Mashatu Game Reserve, Botswana
side of the river.

Contents

Foreword

South Africa has been blessed with remarkable landscapes and hugely impressive rivers. However, of the many rivers, none is so impressive and well-known as the mighty Limpopo River, made famous by Rudyard Kipling's phrase, 'the great grey-green, greasy Limpopo River, all set about with fever-trees'. Just under 1 800 kilometres away on the Highveld, the river begins as a polluted and abused fountain under a developed and industrialised city, however, it ultimately shapes some of the most beautiful, spectacular and unique landscapes in the county.

The roots of the book, *River of Gold*, stretch back decades, and follow the adventures of three passionate naturalists. It encompasses years of study and careful observation of the river system and with it reveals many of its secrets. The passion for this river and in-depth knowledge, experiences and companionship of the authors makes this book unforgettable. The powerful and compelling stories entice readers to share in the journey of this magnificent river from its source in Johannesburg, to a beach at the mouth of the river where it enters the Indian Ocean in Mozambique.

The three authors, Clive Walker, Peter Norton and Michael Gardner have an obvious, infectious passion for this unique river, and provide wonderful insights into the culture, history and ecosystems, as well as the different creatures encountered along the journey. They also share with us fascinating stories of adventure and comradeship.

No words can do justice to describe the majestic Limpopo River, with its breathtaking scenery and diverse flora and fauna. Its impact on the senses is so striking, that this area leaves one with a long-lasting impression and an uncontrollable desire to return. The sunsets too are stunning, with the superbly silhouetted Mashatu trees lingering in the evening light – a truly spiritual experience. This, coupled with contrasting seasons, ensures an ever-changing, ever-rewarding experience, with its often harsh, unforgiving landscapes. The superbly written book captures the mood of the Limpopo and her landscapes. The authors' attention to detail is boldly, yet sensitively, portrayed along the journey.

Our country's rivers are currently under severe threat to pollution and overexploitation, with many classified as threatened or critically threatened. The future of water in South Africa depends on a complete understanding

OPPOSITE: A large fever-tree, *Acacia xanthophloea*, graces the bank of the Limpopo River in the well-known and loved north-eastern Tuli Game Reserve of Botswana.

of the complexities of where it begins and ultimately ends, in all its facets. It is hoped that this book will encourage a more sensible use and understanding of water, and that it will instil a sense of pride for those of us, who, as South Africans, have been entrusted with the honour of conserving and protecting our natural resources for generations to come.

Many books are produced every year, yet few leave the reader with such holistic insight into a subject. *River of Gold* fills a gap in the literature, through the manner in which the unique nature and personality of the river is illustrated. A great overview of the river is provided and I believe it will whet any reader's appetite. This book is compelling, informative and delightful, adding perspective, information and personal highlights throughout. I would like to congratulate all who participated in bringing it to life, and I invite you, the reader, to savour and enjoy this remarkable journey.

Dr Duncan MacFadyen
Manager: Research and Conservation
E Oppenheimer & Son
October 2015

Preface

The Limpopo River's most southern tributary rises in the heart of the City of Gold, Johannesburg, a city with the richest gold deposits in the world. Gold was discovered in 1886 in what was essentially open grassland with scattered bush-clad hillslopes that are bisected by ridges from west to east which became known as the 'Ridge of White Water' – Witwatersrand in Dutch. The 'white water' was a reference to the white quartzite rock from the outflow of water, which glistened in the sun. The Witwatersrand drains two of South Africa's most iconic rivers, the Orange to the south-west and the Limpopo to the north.

It is generally assumed that the Crocodile River is the main source of the Limpopo and there is no doubt about that, certainly in terms of volume of water. However, the Jukskei is in fact the most southern limit of any river that makes up the Limpopo. The Crocodile River rises to the west of Johannesburg high up on a ridge near the train station of Witpoortjie near Roodepoort.

From its source to the sea in Mozambique, the Limpopo River is some 1 750 kilometres long. The river shares a border with three countries: South Africa and Botswana before it enters Mozambique.

Today, over 82 per cent of South Africa's rivers are classified as 'threatened'. Of these, 44 per cent are critically threatened. These figures come from a report published in 2005, the year my co-authors (Peter Norton and Michael Gardner) and I came together with the object of researching a book on the Limpopo River.

Peter Norton was born in Pietermaritzburg and went to school in both Cape Town and Johannesburg. He is an ecologist by training, with a PhD in zoology from the University of Stellenbosch and a former deputy director with the Eastern Cape Department of Conservation. He went on to specialise in integrated tourism development planning. Peter is what I would describe as a quintessential 'naturalist'. He is interested in everything and anything to do with nature and proved to be a wonderful travelling companion, whether diving in the freezing-cold, clear waters of the Eye of Marico, searching for Smuts House at Poachers Corner in Mapungubwe National Park, avoiding foraging elephant or cooking prawns in the pouring rain on the beach of Praia Sepúlveda on the Mozambique coast. He has travelled the coastal regions of Mozambique and is particularly familiar with Mapungubwe National Park, having conducted the proposal for World Heritage Site listing.

Michael Gardner was born in Johannesburg and was, for a period of 11 years, living and working in Rhodesia (Zimbabwe) later rising swiftly to the position of director of Rhodesia National Tourism under the Smith Government. He travelled extensively in the south-eastern area of the country and is very familiar with the Gonarezou National Park. He went on to establish his own canoeing safari operation in 1983 on Lake Kariba and canoe trails down below the dam wall along the Lower Zambezi. He was the first registered canoe guide in Zimbabwe. He certainly knows something about 'rivers'. He specialised as a travel consultant for many years, having advised the tourism sector of the Limpopo Province on various projects and assisted Peter in the compilation of the proposal of the Mapungubwe National Park as a World Heritage Site.

As the third author I was born in Johannesburg and spent my youth and a good portion of my adult life in the shadow of the Ridge of White Water. The Jukskei of my youth was more of a stormwater drain and, while it could be very dangerous in times of floods, it nevertheless was a fun place to muck about in at Gillooly's Farm. As I grew older in the '50s, it was where we watered our horses on our long rides from Bedfordview to the Modderfontein dynamite plant over miles of grassland haunted by guineafowl, grass-owls and the occasional antelope.

As authors we set out to study the river in detail and to bring out as much of its history as we could unravel, from hunters, traders, explorers, travellers, poachers, visionaries, conservationists, writers, and those who would dare the unknown. This story has had a long gestation for all of us – starting back as it did in 2005 – and for the three of us it represents a long quest to know it better. Each of us has had our own special reason and relationship with the river and we came together to pool our knowledge, experiences and companionship.

At the outset we all agreed only one of us should write the text and this important task was taken on by Peter. Between the two of us we have captured the river, in all its moods and beauty, in pictures complimented by my sketches. We felt in order to do it justice it was most important to traverse the entire river from its source to the sea. And what a journey that has been.

From the commencement of this journey in preparing this book, two of us have travelled the river from the source to sea. Not – I hasten to add – in one single journey but rather many journeys over a period of some three years; in Peter's case and mine on a number of occasions together, on many occasions alone or with family and friends.

The co-authors and I have made the most difficult part of the river journey together, from the Limpopo River Mouth to the Pafuri Border Post. This route is certainly or, more correctly, not by any stretch of the imagination, a known traveller's route. We travelled for nearly a week, often at no more than 20 kilometres an hour and through soft powdery sand. This is part of the route Captain Frederick Elton took in 1870 and more importantly over the area where the Voortrekker leader Van Rensburg and his party were massacred in July of 1836. To navigate we relied on the river always being on our right and marvelled at the lack of anything remotely

describable as a road, following mostly cattle sledge tracks. Little, if any, wildlife was observed bar the tracks of a small herd of elephant.

Our journey commenced in July 2006 on the beach at the mouth of the river where it enters the Indian Ocean. Michael and I had travelled up together from the Waterberg and met up with Peter, Di, his wife at the time, and their four sons, Gary, Colin, Tony and Eric who had proceeded us by a week and travelled down together to the mouth of the river. On a high dune overlooking the mouth stands a lighthouse, the Monte Belo, built in 1914 to guide coastal steamers coming into the mouth. The lighthouse is no longer in use because the mouth of the river is now completely silted over, preventing any movement up the river. Beyond the mouth in a sheltered cove, lined with graceful palm trees, one finds Port Captain. This place-name was taken from the original Port Captain who once controlled craft coming in and out of the river.

At this point we waded into the river and Peter filled a small bottle of water which we held up to the light but sensibly elected not to sip. This, for us, was a symbolic gesture – similar to the one described in the introduction to the human history of the river as first seen by Vasco da Gama in 1498.

Water is, after all, life. Without it we as humans would die within three days. Water is, according to our constitution, a basic human right. Water is about rivers, wetlands, catchments, biodiversity and now, more ominously, climate change, which if we abuse or choose to ignore, we do so at our own peril.

If this work achieves one thing – to bring to a wide audience an appreciation of rivers and wetlands, and the vital role they play in the lives of people and biodiversity – we as authors would count the task as most worthwhile.

Clive Walker
October 2015

ABOVE: The author, Clive Walker, with a group of trailists on the banks of a very swollen Limpopo River on the Botswana side in 1977.

FOLLOWING SPREAD: Zebra and impala come to water in the Pitsani River in the Mashatu Game Reserve. It was at this spot that Bryce built a store before the turn of the 19th century near the river along the very route used by the Zeedeberg Coach Company en route to Fort Tuli in present day Zimbabwe.

CHAPTER 1

Introduction
to the
Limpopo

ABOVE: The authors from left to right: Peter Norton, Mike Gardner (holding the bottle of Limpopo water) and Clive Walker near the mouth of the river in Mozambique.

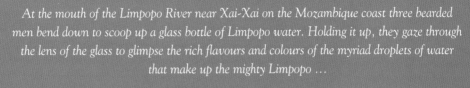

At the mouth of the Limpopo River near Xai-Xai on the Mozambique coast three bearded
men bend down to scoop up a glass bottle of Limpopo water. Holding it up, they gaze through
the lens of the glass to glimpse the rich flavours and colours of the myriad droplets of water
that make up the mighty Limpopo …

A drop of perspiration from the thousands of miners, many from the Limpopo Valley in Mozambique,
toiling underground in stifling conditions to dig the rich gold of the Witwatersrand.

A drop of crystal clear lime-rich water from the dolomite caves of the Cradle of Humankind, which
has yielded the richest collection of fossils of early man yet found anywhere in the world.

A drop of jerepigo sweet wine, and the rich stories of Herman Charles Bosman
and his beloved Marico River.

A drop of dry, sandy Shashe River that was once filled by the mighty waters of the Okavango and
Zambezi rivers, which completely dominated the trickle of the Limpopo before a major shift of the
Gondwana plate cut off the rivers, leaving a wide sandy riverbed.

A drop of Mapungubwe gold from the Shashe River confluence, moulded into the exquisite Golden
Rhino, now recognised as a symbol of the first sophisticated kingdom in southern Africa.

A drop of contemplation as Jan Smuts enjoyed a secluded Limpopo sunset, and thought through his
concept of Holism which shows how all things are interrelated.

A drop of magic mountain water from the sacred lakes of Fundudzi and the Venda highlands.

A drop of cheap grog drunk by the rag-tag of dubious but interesting characters, poachers and
smugglers, giving the Makuleke area a reputation as 'Crooks' Corner'.

A sniff of high explosive from a landmine hidden in the sand around Mapai to prevent a surprise
attack by the 'Rhodesian' or South African forces during the Mozambican civil war.

A drop of human blood from the Van Rensburg Trek on their way to Sofala, before they were
massacred by Soshangane's impis as they prepared to cross the Limpopo River near Combomune.

A drop of lala wine drunk by Ngungunyane as he calmly waited to be captured by the Portuguese
under a marula tree at Chaimite, marking the end of the powerful Gaza Kingdom.

A drop of tears for the thousands of Mozambicans killed by rising Limpopo floodwaters, from which
many were dramatically rescued by being hoisted into a helicopter.

A drop of compassion for the thousands of slaves shipped out from this part of Mozambique during the
eighteenth and nineteenth centuries, breaking up families and shattering their dignity.

PREVIOUS SPREAD: Early dawn at Mapungubwe from the south bank of the river with Zimbabwe across the water.

The Limpopo River

The Limpopo River has many moods, and a rich story to tell. We have tried to capture some of this diversity, following the 1 750-kilometre course of the river from its origins in the Witwatersrand to the mouth on the Mozambique coast.

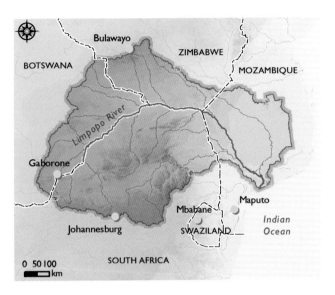

After the summer rains across the catchment areas which cover four southern African countries – Botswana, Zimbabwe, South Africa and Mozambique – it finally drains into the Indian Ocean near Xai-Xai. After it has gathered up all this water it presents a formidable sight and can wreak havoc in eastern Mozambique, as our story will tell. Giant trees can be broken loose from the soil, plunging down ever widening banks rushing headlong downstream. The changing geology of the river basin through which it has carved its way, long before the Zambezi flowed over the present-day Victoria Falls, is fascinating. Perhaps difficult to believe but true. It can be as smooth as silk, and violent enough to deter the bravest, often very dry with water reduced to pools or thin slivers as it disappears beneath shimmering sand, only to emerge far, further downstream.

Magnificent towering sandstone formations follow the river's length in the north, interspersed by jutting basalt and great granite outcrops that dot the border between South Africa and Botswana, the flood plains of Mozambique and the high coastal dunes at its mouth.

The following pages will reveal far more; not least the wonderful accounts of travellers, explorers, local people with ancient histories, soldiers, artists, hunters and today's conservationists who strive to protect the unique biodiversity and landscapes of this iconic river.

Reading makes explorers of all of us even if, for most, we have never left the comfort of our homes.

OPPOSITE: Buti, a local Motswana guide from one of the lodges on the Botswana side, gazes across the swollen Limpopo River after the onset of the rains.

Why 'Limpopo'?

The origin of the name *Limpopo* is unclear. The British and Dutch/Afrikaans settlers have always used this name, but only for the stretch of the river after the confluence of the Crocodile and Marico. The Tswana apparently do not make this distinction, and have always called both the *Crocodile* and *Limpopo* the '*Oori*'. It is interesting that, even though the name Limpopo seems to be a corruption of the local names, it has now been widely accepted to the point that the black-dominated former Northern Province government asked for the province's name to be changed to Limpopo Province.

The following gives an understanding of the names that were used:

In 1939, Carel Birkby,[1] author and South African foreign correspondent during World War II, describes a possible theory, according to the recognised authority on South African place-names, Rev. Charles Pettman. He believes that it comes from the Zulu phrase *uku popoza*, meaning to rush. However, Joshua Sitole, Birkby's Zulu guide and philosopher, 'disputes the authority, and says that "*uku popoza*" means to come roistering along after a beer-drink, which is an apt simile for the Limpopo as it comes down when the heavy rains begin and the sluggish pools of water swirl full …'

He claims that 'the river owes its name to the Zulu phrase "*Ulimu popo!*" which means "Tongue, beware!" [possibly related to] some taboo about talking of the river. This Limpopo River, besides being called the *Crocodile* … is called the *Inhampura*, the *Bembe*, the *Miti*, the *River of Gold* and the *River of Kings*.'

Bulpin, in his *Lost Trails of the Transvaal* published in 1965, wrote 'Then, when the first Europeans arrived, they apparently picked up what seems to have been an Ndebele name for the river *Limpopo* or *Lemphopho* (River of the Waterfall) and this name has been recorded for ever on the maps of the world.' He further mentioned that the Tswana people knew it as *Noka-eya Udi*, the *River of Steep Banks*.

The southern reaches of the river downstream of the Motloutse River are indeed steep. The Venda people refer to the river as the *Vhembe*, the gatherer, while various other tribes in Mozambique call it the *Mete*, the swallower. Both names bear reference to the destructive nature of the river. Bulpin throws some light on the present-day name for the river by suggesting that 'when the first Europeans arrived, they apparently picked up what seems to have been an Ndebele name for the river *Limpopo* or *Lemphopho*, *River of the Waterfall*.'

While researching the origin of the word in 1967 in the original Africana Library in downtown Johannesburg, the following was recorded from Birkby in 1939 by one of the authors: 'Written in Setswana, Limpopo would become "Dimphopho"; however, all early missionaries wrote "L" for "D" whenever "D" was followed by an "I".'

Captain William Cornwallis Harris[2] (later Sir William) was an Indian army officer who conducted a hunting expedition in 1836 and wrote about the 'Limpopo' from the Magaliesberg onwards to roughly the Tropic of Capricorn. In other words, what is now known as the Crocodile from Magaliesberg to Olifants Drift was called Limpopo in his day. He was an accomplished artist and writer and left one of the most detailed accounts of his exploits of travel and particularly of hunting the elephant, hippo and buffalo near the Limpopo River. Only 500 copies of his first publication were printed in 1840 followed by two further editions which rank today among the most valuable and sought-after items of Africana.

Erskine[3] 1869: 'They have still another name for the river here "Meti" which adds one more to the list, Limpopo, Krokodil, Ouri, or Bembe; and, as my observations seem to point out the Inhampura River's mouth as the outlet, the list may be still further increased. In ancient geography the river is called "Spirito Sancto".'

Thomas Baines, the English-born artist and explorer, was familiar with the southern reaches of the Limpopo and even had a drift named after him between the border posts of Zanzibar and Platjan. Upon returning from one of his expeditions in 1871 when close to the Motloutse River, a wide tributary of the Limpopo, he recorded: 'we saw hills on the south side of the Limpopo or L'Oorie, as it is called.'

Erskine[4] said: 'In the afternoon we passed the mouth of the Limpopo, Bembe, Miti or Inhampura River … The Limpopo is usually called Miti by the Zulus [i.e. Shangaans], Bembe by the Baloyia and Tongas, and Ouri by the Basuto.'

Another reference is by Ferreira[5], translated from Montanha's 1855 diary: 'After sunset we set up camp in the forest under some large trees near a large river that the blacks called the Bembe River (Rio do Ouro) … The Bembe River is also called Rio do Ouro (Gold River), Vhembe, Crocodillos, Inhampura and Limpopo. Vasco da Gama gave the river the name Rio de Cobre (Copper River) because the people he met at the river mouth wore copper ornaments.'

More recently, Ralushai[6] recorded in 2001 that: 'Vhembe … is a Venda word for the river Limpopo. According to Adv. Mathole Motshekga, a Northern Sotho speaking lawyer … the Northern Sotho people use Bêpê for Limpopo River. Bêpê is derived from the Venda term Vhembe … In predominantly Tswana speaking areas (i.e. in Botswana and North West Province), they use the term hodi or odi for the Limpopo River … As far as the name Limpopo is concerned, we found nobody who knew its origin and meaning around the Mapungubwe area.'

Why is the River Important?

The Limpopo River has for long been linked to gold (see box on page 24), from the earliest kingdoms to the riches of present-day Johannesburg, known to many as 'Egoli' or the City of Gold, the origin of which may well have arisen from the early mineworkers who came from Portuguese East Africa (Mozambique).

For Europeans it was a border and an important frontier. Initially the Highveld was the frontier, but once the Voortrekkers had left the Eastern Cape and arrived in the far north, the Limpopo marked the transition into 'Wild Africa'. To a large extent, it has remained so ever since.

This was not the case for the early black tribes of southern Africa, though, as they moved freely backwards and forwards across the river, making use of its extensive floodplains for agriculture, and regarding it as the centre of their territory rather than a dividing line. The Venda still live on both sides of the river.

For Cecil John Rhodes and the empire builders it was not seen as an obstacle, but as a frontier that needed to be crossed in their quest to 'paint the map red' from the Cape to Cairo. Thus the occupation of Rhodesia by the Pioneer Column and later the Beit Bridge carrying the railway northwards were two key achievements during the Rhodes era.

For many hunters the Limpopo signified the major wildlife area of the country, and was always a route through to these areas, particularly for elephant hunting, well into the twentieth century.

ABOVE: The city skyline of Johannesburg, looking south from the northern ridge of 'white water', one of a number of prominent outcrops that characterise Johannesburg.

Farmers, explorers and hunters entering the middle and lower Limpopo Valley required a change of mindset, and particularly a change of transport routes, because the tsetse fly belt stretched in an arc around the Highveld, penetrating almost to Rustenburg. This was the case right up to the end of the nineteenth century when the 'fly' retreated as the wildlife, their food source, were decimated first by hunting and then by the Rinderpest epidemic of 1896–97 which wiped out the cattle.

The political 'rules of the game' were always quite different on the 'other side of the Limpopo'. For almost the whole of the twentieth century, the area south of the Limpopo was dominated by Europeans and their mine-based commercial activity, with a strong feeling that the whites 'owned' the land, whereas to the north there was more of a feeling of being 'occupiers'.

For Victorian England the Limpopo was a strange river that 'didn't have a beginning and didn't have an end'. On the one hand, it only became what they called the Limpopo once the Crocodile and Marico rivers came together, as is the case today. On the other hand, for several decades there was disagreement as to where the Limpopo entered the sea, and it was only in 1868 that St Vincent Erskine[7] could confirm that the mouth was neither at Delagoa Bay nor near Inhambane, but a relatively small river mouth in between at Inhampura.

The Limpopo has always been associated with hunting, and for generations the Limpopo Valley has been recorded as one of the prime hunting lands of southern Africa. In the early 1800s, 'there was good sport to be had' in the Magaliesberg area, but for the rest of the century the hunting lands gradually retreated downstream as the big game was hunted out, like a tide going out in the Limpopo Valley. By the early 1900s, game was scarce as far as Crooks' Corner, but there was still good hunting in Mozambique nearby. As people realised that they could do something about this, the tide started turning. The first conservation initiatives, most notably the reserves that became the Kruger National Park, allowed game populations to build up in substantial areas, which gradually increased over the first half of the century. From the 1960s onwards private game farms gathered momentum, and 'the tide came in' with game rapidly repopulating the Limpopo Valley. Hunting by both overseas trophy hunters and domestic 'biltong' hunters provided the economic drivers needed to return the Limpopo Valley to prime hunting lands of South Africa by the end of the twentieth century.

The river itself is *not* a navigation channel, such as the other major rivers of Africa – the Nile, Niger, Congo and Zambezi. In spite of early attempts to prove otherwise, only the last 50 kilometres from Xai-Xai to the mouth have carried any meaningful amount of riverine traffic; there are only a few other records of trips of any length on the river, and these have all been by adventurers of one sort or another.

For more than a thousand years the Limpopo River has been a lifeline for farmers, bringing irrigation water and rich soil to an otherwise parched land. However, this is when it is in its benign mood. Every decade or so the river becomes angry, and raging

River of Gold

ABOVE: Golden light from the setting sun bathes the slowly retreating waters of the Limpopo River.

The Portuguese called the Limpopo the *Rio do Ouro*, the River of Gold, probably because they believed that it would lead them to the Land of Ophir, the mystical country of King Solomon's

mines and untold riches in gold. They were right in many ways, but not in the way that they expected. The surface deposits on the Zimbabwe plateau provided enough gold for it to be a key symbol of wealth for Great Zimbabwe, but they were pretty much exhausted by the time the Portuguese arrived on the Mozambique coast in the late fifteenth century.

Gold was the key symbol of wealth in Great Zimbabwe's predecessor, the Kingdom of Mapungubwe. The Golden Rhino (see Chapter 4) found at Mapungubwe has got to be the most important icon of this early period in the history of southern Africa. The rich collection of the golden sceptre, golden bowl and thousands of golden beads were clearly important symbols of power. Unfortunately most of Great Zimbabwe's gold was robbed and melted down by avaricious fortune hunters, including a company Cecil John Rhodes was a shareholder of! Who knows what treasures could otherwise have become further icons for the people of this part of Africa.

Gold continued to be seen as a symbol of power after the collapse of Great Zimbabwe, and the ruins of Thulamela near Crooks' Corner in northern Kruger Park yielded several gold beads floodwaters exert a heavy toll on agricultural lands, equipment, livestock and human life for the farmers living on the floodplain. The worst on record were the dramatic floods of 2000, where high rainfall, tropical cyclones and poor catchment management all came together to create a catastrophe that made headline news across the world. However, floods almost as high as these have always been part of the picture.

FOLLOWING SPREAD: A large fever-tree graces the high river bank on the Botswana side of the Limpopo River seen here in flood.

and a golden wire bracelet from the grave of a royal princess.

The real gold wealth was only discovered much later. There were several minor gold rushes in South Africa in the second half of the nineteenth century, one of which was a titter of excitement caused when PJ Marais found traces of gold in the Crocodile and Jukskei rivers, close to their confluence, in 1853. This was the first evidence of what was to become the greatest gold treasure house in the world, the Witwatersrand Main Reef.

Marais searched for years without success, and then more and more people started finding traces of gold, but only in marginal quantities. In 1886, George Harrison, a quiet and rather uneducated prospector and carpenter, found the Main Reef on the farm Langlaagte, which precipitated the main gold rush to the Rand. Many of the Randlords, that 'ambitious, eccentric crew of adventurers, magnates and financiers'[8] who made fortunes over the next decade, built grand suburbs in the new area of Doornfontein and its surrounds. These were established on the farm of the same name, situated right at the headwaters of the Jukskei River, the most southerly tributary of the Limpopo River.

In just over a century more than 50 000 tonnes of gold have been mined in these reefs, nearly a third of all the gold production in history. Although most of the reef is just to the south of the watershed that divides the waters of the Limpopo and Vaal rivers, the southern part has remained mostly a mining area, and the fabulous wealth generated has been carried across the watershed to the residential and commercial suburbs of Johannesburg, on the headwaters of the many streams that feed the Limpopo River.

Downstream of Thulamela the impact of gold is indirect. Up to 80 000, mostly black mine labourers have been recruited each year by the Witwatersrand Native Labour Association (popularly known as Wenela), and later its successor, The Employment Bureau of Africa (TEBA). A substantial number have always come from the Limpopo Valley, and the accumulated effect of thousands of labourers' wages, little as they were, for over a century has fundamentally improved the livelihoods of those living in the lower Limpopo Valley area. Studies have shown that this additional wealth plays a substantial role in families' ability to recover after the Limpopo River comes down in a devastating flood, as it does at regular intervals.

The story of the Limpopo River clearly has a thread of gold running through it, all the way from its source to the sea.

Writings about the Limpopo

Many people have had a relationship with the river and have been in a position to document this – important people, ordinary people, hunters, traders, politicians, soldiers, conservationists, journalists, artists. Sometimes the river inspires them and sometimes it terrifies them, sometimes it impresses them, and sometimes it disappoints them …

Most of the earliest accounts are from early explorers, traders and hunters who left a rich legacy of narrative and a few drawings of what the Limpopo was like in the early days. Since most of them originated from that peculiarly 'British penchant for idealising the flamboyant gentleman amateur braving individual hardship as the imperial spearhead'[9], there is a distinctly British bias in the historical accounts. Nevertheless, this is tempered with scarcer, but equally rich, accounts from Voortrekkers, missionaries, a cosmopolitan group of hunters, Portuguese navigators, traders and priests, and oral history from the black tribes of the region.

The banks of the river have been used as a trading route since long before the white men came, but there is very little information available from this early period. We have to try to understand the river by working with whatever historical accounts we can find. Tales of the early, mostly British, hunters paint a picture of the Crocodile River and the Limpopo up to the Shashe confluence in the mid-nineteenth century. The Marico River in the early 1900s is immortalised in the wonderfully rich writings of Herman Charles Bosman.[10] The middle section from the Shashe confluence to Crooks' Corner has just a few descriptions of specific sites on the river, as well as Captain Frederick Elton's journey on the Limpopo. The accounts pertaining to the Pafuri section of Kruger Park are well summarised in an important Afrikaans work, *Neem uit die Verlede* by U de V Pienaar, and there are a range of writings about the river in Mozambique, including historical accounts, explorers' journeys – particularly that of Erskine – and some hunting accounts.

By far the best-known words penned about the Limpopo, at least in English, describe it as the 'Great, grey-green, greasy Limpopo River all set about with fever-trees' from the story 'The Elephant's Child' by poet and writer Rudyard Kipling.[11] It is not clear where on the river he was inspired to write these immortal words, but there is some evidence that 'in 1898 Rhodes arranged for Kipling to make a visit up to the territory of Rhodesia … and it was on this expedition that Kipling saw "the great, grey-green, greasy Limpopo".'[12] However, it is likely that he went up by train – the line to Bulawayo had been completed the year before. Unless he made a special trip to it he may not have actually seen the river, and relied instead on descriptions from hunters and explorers who knew the river well.

Some of the other major rivers of Africa, such as the Zambezi, Nile and Okavango, each have several books written about them already. For the Limpopo there are only two books that focus on the river itself. In the 1930s journalist Carel Birkby planned a canoe trip from Beit Bridge to the sea, but this trip remained a pipe dream. He drove most of it, and published his experiences in *Limpopo Journey* (1939), which is an account of travelling in the general Limpopo area, with some rich descriptions of the river itself, especially in the Mozambique section, but also casting the net very wide to include stories of people and events quite far from the river, such as Maleboch on Blouberg and Mujaji near Tzaneen. A more recent 1965 book by Walter Battiss simply called *Limpopo*, can perhaps best be described as a celebration of an artist's relationship with a section of the river. His rich, almost surreal, words may be 'over-the-top' for some, but contain descriptions that anyone who has spent time on the river should be able to identify with (see box below).

Walter Battiss and the Limpopo[13]

Battiss, born in the then Orange Free State in 1906, was one of South Africa's most acclaimed and colourful artists. A lecturer and writer, he travelled parts of the Limpopo and later wrote of his exploits in his 1965 book, *Limpopo*. He clearly loved the river from his vivid descriptions of it. For him the river was 'The background of the spiritual drama of my life'.

He preferred the Limpopo to the Nile although the Nile's great delta impressed him. What fascinated him most was that the Limpopo in winter 'disappears and shrivels up like a dying plant'. And then after the summer rains it re-emerges and 'carves itself a home in the sands once more'. He best sums up his feelings about the river and its abundant life: 'Sometimes in the bush, the world is full of birds. The sky is merely space between the birds; trees cease to exist as trees but as spaces in between birds.'

He was very aware of the abundance of nature around him during this time spent along the river:

'Sometimes, pinned close to the earth in my camp bed I seem to be in communication with the secrets of the underground. The aura of the earth envelopes one, I slide through subterranean palaces of light and swim in rivers of curling vapour.

'Sometimes all nature lies suspended from the sky, a heavy, solid sky to which earth's forms are tied, fixed, anchored and hanging. The tall aapiesboom and the yellow fever tree creep down from the sky and loosely connect themselves with the shimmering, melting, vaporous earth.'

Tales of Five Boatmen

To really experience the river one needs to be on it to feel its immense, silent surges of power when it is in full spate. Nothing stirs except the incessant drone of cicadas in the dense riverine undergrowth that flank both banks. Magnificent trees of all descriptions abound with the ever-present fish-eagle surveying the water. Occasional bushbuck may be seen and the Egyptian geese, annoyed by our intrusion, take flight downstream. Time is the only element that stands still here. The river moves forward relentlessly and silently, which is exhilarating not least because of the sight of a hippo's head disappearing and heading into the unknown. So we begin our journey down the Limpopo with five stories of boatmen and their companions who travelled large sections of the river in various types of craft, spread over 132 years:

- In 1870 Frederick Elton built a sailing boat and wanted to prove that the river was navigable from the Shashe confluence to the sea (see box on page 32).
- In 1924 'Brownie' Ramke, his companion and a dog paddled from Beit Bridge to Guija in a wood-and-iron canoe, on an adventure trip (see box on page 34).
- In 1962 Willem van Riet and his friends canoed from Buffelsdrift to the mouth, in his quest to 'conquer' all the major rivers of southern Africa (see box on page 38).
- In 1998 Sean Waller and a companion paddled in inflatable canoes on a relaxed adventure trip from Pafuri to Chokwe, which turned into a nightmare when his companion became very ill (see box on page 43).
- In 2002 Robert Perkins, a filmmaker from the USA, paddled from the Crocodile–Marico confluence to Xai-Xai, leaving out the rocky stretches below Mabalel and the Limpopo Gorge below Malala Drift (see box on page 46).

In spite of exhaustive research, we have not found any other accounts of people who have travelled more than short sections on the river. Clive Walker was one of them. He pioneered a short canoe trail from the border post at Pont Drift to the confluence of the Shashe and Limpopo rivers, a distance of some 25 kilometres, in 1977 as part of the five-day Ivory Trail which had occurred annually for over 13 years using sturdy Canadian-style fibreglass canoes, seating three participants. With good rains canoeing was usually possible for up to six months, providing breathtaking views of the river while keeping a lookout for wildlife. No incident ever occurred involving crocodile or hippo. Most had been shot out in those days, although on rare occasions canoes were capsized due to the powerful current depositing the occupants into the river. Canoes and occupants were recovered although the odd bird book, towel, suntan lotion and tennis shoe was lost in the 'great, grey-green' depths.

The rest of the many stories and experiences all refer to people travelling on land *along* the river, which will be dealt with in the relevant sections.

ABOVE: Willem van Riet, from a viewpoint in Mapungubwe National Park, points out a rocky point on an island in the Limpopo to Clive Walker, which he scaled on his epic 'canoe' journey down the Limpopo in 1962.

LEFT: Sean Waller paddles his inflatable canoe on a remote stretch of the river in Mozambique in 1998.

In July 1870 Captain Frederick Elton persuaded the London and Limpopo Mining Company to help him finance an expedition to see whether the Limpopo was navigable to the sea, and therefore avoiding the expensive and time-consuming transport of goods from Natal, through Potchefstroom, all the way up to the mine in Zimbabwe. He set off from the confluence of the Limpopo and Shashe rivers in a 'flat-bottomed boat, 13 feet long, with masts, sails, oars, etc …' The boat had been constructed on the Tati and carried all the way down to the Limpopo, first by ox wagon, and the last more than 200 kilometres on foot, with up to 20 porters.

The following extracts from his report on the journey to the Royal Geographical Society in November 1871 give insights into his personality, resourcefulness and prejudices, and at the same time give glimpses of what the people and the river were like more than 130 years ago … Elton was correct in one respect that the Limpopo was navigable but neither he nor Thomas Baines knew that it was for only a moderate distance from the mouth inland. Baines knew only the southern reaches of the Limpopo.

'The idea of making a voyage down the Limpopo first struck me on seeing the river in January 1870, and subsequently at Mangwe in the Matabele country, I discussed my plans with Mr Baines, F.R.G.S. who was sanguine to the results of such an exploration, his theory being that the waters of the "Usabia and Limpopo joined and emptied themselves into the sea by a river which would prove of navigable utility …"'

He went so far as to obtain the patronage of Lobengula, King of the Matabele:

'… No-Bengule [!] promised to forward my projected journey, as far as my line of travel passed through the tribes over which he held any power …'

Prior to setting off on his epic but short river journey, he recorded his impressions of the Makalaka people they encountered in present-day Zimbabwe.

'The men possess a considerable number of guns, and depend mainly on them to supply the villages with meat, all ivory killed in the chase becoming the property of the Chiefs, who pay an annual tribute of tusks to the Matabele …

'The salutation of the Makalaka consists in loudly slapping the hands together, after which snuff is passed round. A silence of some minutes ensues, and eventually the business of the visit is gradually broached by a series of questions, involving the relation of the stranger's whole personal history and future plans.

'On the 12th July, I prophesied the eclipse of the moon, which was witnessed to the greatest advantage, the night being clear and fine, and then on the following morning told the chief that I could read his thoughts … and that as I foresaw the eclipse, so I could readily foresee that the Matabele would punish his tribe unless this nonsense came to an end. After this, I had no further trouble with him …

'At dawn on the 1st August, I began my voyage, Selika's men shrieking with delight and excitement, at the sight of the first boat that had even been launched on the upper waters of "the great river" …'

On the second day after having entered the Limpopo at its confluence with the Shashe River, the sight of the present-day Mapungubwe National Park, he recorded the first and second-last adventure on the river:

'On the 2nd … coming suddenly round a

bend, the boat was driven down by the stream, and upset under the wide spreading branches of a large tree … I lost all my blankets, waterproof sheet, thick overcoat and cooking utensils, and my store of tobacco and sugar was entirely spoilt. Irreparable misfortunes!'

Worse was still to come when on the sixth day he recorded the following, not unlike Willem van Riet and his companions 92 years later. While terrifyingly similar, the experience did not end Van Riet's expeditions on the river as later recorded:

'… The increasing roar of distant waters … was a danger warning of ominous portent …

'Twenty yards' walk opened up a spectacle well calculated to make us shudder at the peril we had so narrowly escaped. A magnificent fall dashed down into a yawning chasm right ahead of the channel where we had stopped … Torrents of pale green water tore through the narrow passage beneath our feet, foaming and breaking in clouds of spray, over huge boulders, syenite and micaceous rocks, intermixed with masses of a reddish-coloured granite rising perpendicularly from the gorge and overtopped by a sombre, columnar wall of basalt …

'[The boat] was swept down the chasm, the wreck finally lodging on a ledge of rocks near our camp, completely knocked to pieces, and of no further service, and I consequently abandoned the *Freeman* – a most unfortunate loss.'

Elton continued his journey, only this time on foot, and left us with some very interesting observations of the local population and a somewhat tainted view of, in his words, the *'Dutchmen'*.

'At another of the nondescript villages to be found on the Limpopo … [we] met with a warm reception from a rude but hospitable population, rich in pumpkins, millet, maize, *dakha* [marijuana], ground nuts and sun-dried locusts … The men are dark, and affect scalp-locks as a prevailing coiffure, carry snuff-gourds, and wear the scantiest loin-cloths of leather as an apology for clothing. They are inseparable from their spears, bows, and poisoned arrows, and never move unarmed from their carefully stockaded villages, which are built on the hillsides under perpendicular cliffs, and in localities well chosen for defence … They dwell in daily dread of their neighbours.

'I beg to state most emphatically that any Englishman can travel in these parts and on the Limpopo, and be well and hospitably received, *as soon as it is seen that he is not a Dutchman*; and the reason alleged by the tribes is "that the Boers make slaves, and the English pay for labour".'

Elton was not the type to give up easily, although he had largely run out of options and all his equipment. The loss of his boat put paid to his dream of confirming the navigability of the Limpopo River. Nonetheless he set out for the coast on foot, which in any event was an epic feat that he made two months after leaving the Tati.

'… Arriving early the next morning in pouring rain at the gates of Lourenço Marques, where the sentry appeared to have some scruples in admitting a party headed by a white man dressed in an old leathern kilt and gaiters, considerably travel-stained, and rather excusably over-excited at his safe arrival at the seaboard.'

Elton later became a renowned artist and author, and the British Vice-Consul in Delagoa Bay. He died of sunstroke in 1877 while returning from an expedition to northern Mozambique and Lake Nyasa, at the age of 37.

Ramke's canoe trip from Beit Bridge to Guija[15]

Wilfred Southey Ramke-Meyer, known to everyone as 'Brownie' Ramke, was a mine engineer at the Messina copper mine, who spent much of his spare time roaming around the bush next to the river, and developed a hankering to boat down the river through the wild virtually unexplored country into Mozambique.

Towards the end of 1921 it was decided to shut the copper mine down and all staff were given notice. Being young and now unemployed, Brownie and a couple of his mates decided it was time to tackle the river. None of them had experience in any sort of river travel or boating, but they finally decided on a flat-bottomed, punt-like craft, which they designed and knocked together in the mine workshop. The idea was that 'in shallow waters it would skim over the top, and not require any portage. In other words just like "sailing down the river on a Sunday afternoon", while we relaxed or read, or darned socks [!] and occasionally shoot something for the pot.'

They set off from Main Drift in February 1922, but it was soon evident that the craft was totally unsuitable for the expedition, having little response to either oars or rudder. All being young and obstinate, they pushed on for 12 days, before finally deciding that hunting and exploring round the Njelele would be far more sensible. While hunting, they received a message that the mine was to be reopened and they would all be re-instated, so they returned to Messina (now known as Musina).

In late 1924 Brownie once again turned his mind to going down the river. This time he designed and built a timber-framed, iron-clad canoe with water-tight compartments and repairable hull, following advice and guidance from a Finn in the office who had experience with kayaks and one of his office boys, Nyasa, from Malawi who had experience with dugouts. Leaks in this iron sheeting were repaired along the trip by soldering.

The only colleague who was crazy enough to go with him was 'Robbie' Robertson, who was not a bushman and had no boating experience, but 'thought a cruise down the river might alleviate that boredom of the mine'. The first 'passenger' was Ms Louis Stubbs in whose honour the boat was named *Louis*. By mid-May all was ready and the stores were assembled. They consisted of coffee, sugar, flour, baking powder, a case of ships biscuits and most importantly 12 bottles of Bertrams brandy. They also took rifles and pistols and a good supply of ammunition. A fox terrier-type dog of doubtful parentage also attached himself to the expedition.

They set off again from Main Drift in May 1925, and all went well up to Malala Drift. There was plenty of water and, other than aggressive, though harmless, attacks by crocodiles, they just let the current take them along, and thought the trip would be a piece of cake. However, the next ten days were totally different. The rapids and rocks were endless. Porterage over the really rough sections was backbreaking and dangerous and the few times they could rope the boat down some of the rapids were equally so. They took seven days to cover the 50 kilometres from Malala Drift to the end of the gorge near Mabiligwe. Some quotes from his account give a feel for this interesting stretch of the river and vividly illustrate the challenges they faced:

'We ran into the big water and paddled sharply right into a bay away from the strong currents. As I lifted my paddle from the water at the end of a stroke it struck hard, and there was a snap of heavy jaws closing. I turned just in time to see the long green snout of a crocodile disappearing below the surface. Fortunately we were paddling fast, and I hit him first, and fortunately too that the bank was close and the whisky handy.

'… At last ahead appeared blue water and a bank of sand, so we got into the boat and let her go, bumps or not. She was already badly dented, some of the stiffening slats were broken and she leaked in every seam, so we figured a few extra knocks would do no harm. The rocks thinned rapidly and the numerous streams converged, when, glory be to Allah, we ran out on a blue river winding over white beds of sand. On the right bank was a native. We called to him and the shock sent him to his knees where he spent the next five minutes raising his hands above his head and saluting us with "*Inkoos*" …

'… Wide glens opened on the stream, great fig trees shaded the banks, birds were legion and grey monkeys chattered at us … It was all like a fairy dream after the hell above.'

When they reached Pafuri they took a break and cleared through the border post. From there on the going was easier, but somehow Robbie got an infection in his hand and found paddling was too painful so it was up to Brownie to do the main work.

They pushed on to get medical attention, and finally they reached Guija which was, by comparison to where they had been, the centre of civilisation. There was a sort of a doctor who butchered Robbie's hand and expressed great enthusiasm at the prospect of amputating it. However, the Portuguese officials sent him on to Lourenço Marques and later Durban where he spent six months in hospital, and lost two fingers, but saved the rest of his hand.

Brownie was in a dilemma as he wanted to continue the trip but the slow-running waters of the Limpopo from that point onwards coupled with the seemingly large number of people didn't look challenging enough. He felt that 'we were through where none had come through before' and he was stimulated by adventure. The Komati was by all accounts a much faster-running and more challenging river. So he accompanied Robbie to the station at Xinavane, and then found a local to accompany him down the Komati.

Brownie returned to Messina, and continued with canoeing adventures on the Vaal, Crocodile and Zambesi, and in the late 1930s followed Louis Trichardt's trail down the Olifants River in a new home-built canoe. However, of all his adventures he considered his trip down the Great Limpopo River as the highlight of his life.

ABOVE: The author Clive Walker pioneered a one-day canoe adventure down the Limpopo River as part of a five-day trail in the Mashatu Game Reserve in the late 1970s. Of course, the river contained enough flow, which in those days was for a period of around six months.

FAR LEFT: The river's most iconic tree, the fever-tree, *Acacia xanthophloea*, made famous by Rudyard Kipling's poem.

Willem van Riet persuaded two university buddies, Jopie Overes and Gavin Pike, and lecturer Ronald Horsham to join him on a trip down the Limpopo in December 1962, as part of his annual quest to navigate as many major southern African rivers as possible. They obtained sponsorship, which allowed them to import four fold-up boats from England.

They planned to start at Thabazimbi, but there was no running water; so they got a lift to Buffelsdrift at the Matlabas River confluence. They struggled for three days in shallow water and managed to keep going because the weirs held back the water just enough for them to paddle in. However, the water level was still dropping, and eventually the river dried up completely. They then got another lift on a truck to the Mokolo River, which, to their relief, was flowing strongly.

From there on all went well for a while, in spite of their first close encounters with hippos. At Martin's Drift they treated themselves to dinner at a little hotel, and were interviewed by the police who had heard there were 'Russian spies along the river'!

They saw three huge crocs at Mabalel, the scene of a Tswana maiden being caught by a croc in Eugène Marais's famous Afrikaans poem *Mabalel*. A short while later they had a truly wild Africa experience when a pack of wild dogs chased a waterbuck right through their camp – the waterbuck got away through the river, where the dogs were too scared to follow.

At Zanzibar they restocked from a small hotel again, and then started immediately with a set of the most difficult rapids and overhanging branches they had had so far. They 'struggled on for about a mile, but then the water disappeared between many huge boulders. Exhausted they gave up and walked back to Zanzibar, where they organised a lift in a truck to the Macloutsi River [correct spelling Motloutse].' This was past the rocky stretch (which is reputed to be 60 kilometres long) and on the edge of the wilderness of the Tuli Game Reserve.

They soon came to Rhodes Drift, where the farmer Pieter Quin invited them in and told them lots of stories about the area. After managing to drag themselves away from his hospitality, they paddled on to the Shashe River, where they stood on Beacon Island and admired the view of the confluence. From there they walked up to visit Mapungubwe.

Two days later they reached the Tolo-Azime Waterfall, which proved to be almost as traumatic for them as it had been for Elton 92 years earlier:

'Unexpectedly we find ourselves in the middle of foaming rapids. It sweeps us onwards. A new element is added to the immediate rumbling of the rapids. Suddenly we realise just like Capt. Elton that this must be the falls. The trees and sharp turns make it impossible to reach the bank, and also hinder the view. Helplessly we sit caught up in the power of the brown water that drags us down like a giant throat. There is no chance of escape, and it begins to look as if we cannot avoid being pushed into the gorge. Suddenly a small inlet appears between the rocks in front of us. We carefully steer the boats into it, and succeed in reaching the bank with a sigh of relief, then run over the rocks to the side of the chasm. Forced together in the ravine in front of us streams of brown muddy water … tumble over the 15 foot [4.5 metre] drop …'

'On our right side is the upper waterfall; in front of our feet thunders a powerful rapid and half-way down there is a further step in the water's path to the large pool at the bottom. On the other side lie granite and other boulders as if they had been scattered by a mighty hand.'

They realised that the only way out was for Willem to swim across the 6-metre gorge with a rope, and pull the others across. At that late stage they found that Ronnie couldn't swim! While admiring his courage in coming so far with them, it put them in a difficult situation. They decided to put Ronnie lying flat in the canoe with all their valuables, and to swing him across the fast-flowing water like a pendulum. Willem takes up the story:

'… Jopie cries: "All OK, pull!" For a moment Ronnie has his doubts, fear of the water clearly in his eyes.

'"No!" he cries and grabs wildly at the rock. Too late I hear Jopie's warning, because I have already started and I pull the canoe into the current with Ronnie's fingers still holding onto the rock. For a moment the canoe hesitates and then the current sweeps it out from under him.

'What happens next takes only a few seconds. Ronnie has hardly disappeared under the water and both Jopie and Gavin dive in. Gavin gets hold of the upside-down canoe and Jopie gets Ronnie.

I rush round a boulder to try to intercept them.

'I have only just reached the water when my foot slips and my momentum carries me into the water. Too late I notice that the others have reached the bank safely. Now I must swim like never before, or I'll go over the waterfall …'

He managed to clamber out, and all had white faces as they realised how close that was. They were all safe, but had lost most of their valuables – cameras, lenses, guns, radio.

To save time, Willem managed to paddle down, shoot a flat-sloping chute and then plunge through the huge standing wave at the bottom. The first time he ended up going down backwards, but he then brought the other canoes down safely. They then left the big pool at the bottom and arrived mud-bespattered at the customs post after dark. 'Oh! These must be the mad guys on the Limpopo …'

They had been on the river for 20 days, and done 620 kilometres, but some chunks had to be done by road. They rested for four days, and Ronnie Horsham withdrew from the expedition, partly because he realised what a responsibility he would be for the others in the tough sections ahead.

As they got closer to the Malala Waterfall, 'The river becomes rougher and more turbulent as we approach the first rapids … I hesitate, but then the current shoots round a boulder and I enter a deep pool. I am safe, but … Jopie, who was right at the back, did not see the rock in time and with a crunch of oars and wood the canoe broke in two.'

Luckily they had already sent for a back-up canoe from Cape Town, and Willem went back to fetch it with just a day lost. This one was less stable than their other canoes, and while joining his mates he was attacked by a croc. He shot over his shoulder with a pistol, but lost his balance and landed in the water. Luckily he managed to empty the water from the boat and climb in unscathed, but it was a nerve-wracking few minutes.

They let the canoes down on ropes through the first narrow, shallow gorge, but then had to porter them around the main Malala Falls.

They had another narrow escape when Gavin capsized just a short distance before the Mahokwe Waterfall, but Willem managed to help him to safety. They portered around this waterfall as well. For a short while the river was quiet, but later they shot rapid after rapid, where Jopie broke a paddle and capsized, wetting some of their equipment and food again. So they had to go to bed hungry.

Once again they let the canoes down the rapids with ropes, to reduce the exhausting porterage.

At Qui-Qui Falls the river was a mass of rocks, and they found a detour. Looking up from an island at the bottom, they saw a rough dyke of rocks, and above it the Kanongha Kop. But they were out of the rapids and into the still water.

They had taken six days to do the 90 kilometres from Beit Bridge, of which the last 25 had taken four days. They had got through where only Ramke had been before.

They paddled through to Pafuri, where they were very happy to get some fresh fruit. Their hunting had been largely unsuccessful, but now their rifle and pistol were sealed by the Border Post, in spite of a letter from the Mozambique Consul in Cape Town. That night they enjoyed the hospitality of Dr De Sousa, the doctor for WNLA (The Witwatersrand Native Labour Association), and his wife, who seldom saw visitors and really looked after them well.

They enjoyed the easy-going route to Mapai where they restocked, and then went on to Guija. Although they saw lots of hippos, they were not bothered particularly by them, until they became too casual, teased a group and were chased by the bull. They also noted that there were few locals along the river until the Olifants River confluence.

Just before the confluence, they stopped at a little store to buy a beer, and were most surprised to find a dinner laid on for them! From the Portuguese owner's broken English they heard that in the 1930s his father had had the honour of entertaining General Jan Smuts on a hunt, and was very impressed by the great man. When he heard that there were South Africans in the area again, after so many years, he made up his mind to treat the canoeists to a meal.

It took them only seven days from Pafuri to Guija, where Willem developed tick-bite fever, and feared he might have to give up as well. However, the local doctor gave him a penicillin injection, and they pushed on.

They didn't particularly enjoy the last stretch, which was scruffy and full of people and their rubbish, and of course the tick-bite fever didn't help. In addition, the slow water and headwind made paddling difficult. While still 120 kilometres from the mouth, they were bothered repeatedly by sharks, one of which bit a hole in Jopie's canoe! They had to paddle very quickly to the side and patch it up.

They carried on and were much relieved to reach Xai-Xai close to the mouth, 1 200 kilometres and 35 days from Thabazimbi.

Forty years later Willem pointed out to Clive Walker from a lofty sandstone outlook in the Mapungubwe National Park where he and his companions had beached their canoes at a large 'island' at the confluence of the Limpopo and Shashe rivers. Willem had climbed up to a beacon where he was able to look back into what years later was to become a national park of considerable significance, both ecologically and culturally. After his epic journey, Willem was himself, years later, to become a board member of the South African National Parks and chairman of the conservation committee. Clive served on the same board and the two had, on a number of occasions, jointly visited the park, including the official opening.

BELOW: The main entry point to Botswana is the bridge crossing over the Limpopo River at Groblersbrug/Martins Drift.

FOLLOWING PAGE: The sandstone cliffs rise up alongside the broad Motloutse River before entering the Limpopo. This river, along with the Shashe, a long time ago once bore the inland waters of Botswana to the Limpopo.

In March 1998 Sean Waller and a fit and adventurous American friend, Carey Anne Spear, decided to take some time off from Pafuri River Camp, which he and his father had built, and try to canoe down the Limpopo River to the Indian Ocean.

The river had been flowing strongly in February when they started planning, but the level had dropped by the time they left, although it was still flowing from bank to bank. The authorities in Kruger Park would not allow Sean to launch his canoes at Crooks' Corner, so they were driven through the Pafuri Border Post and then launched their two inflatable 'crocs' a few kilometres downstream.

It was a more relaxed exploration trip than some of the others described earlier, and there was no race against time. Sean and Carey decided to linger at whatever spot took their fancy, and try to interact with the locals. A quote from Sean's diary captures the mood:

'We were awoken this morning by the rhythmic splashing of an old man punting his dugout across the river. The horizon glowed from the sun, still half an hour from rising. The old man pulled his boat up in front of us, tipped his hat in greeting and, without a second glance, ducked into the bush and was gone … When the sun rose, three women appeared out of the bush, with shy smiles laid down fresh green mealies and without a word melted back into the bush. We are in heaven!'

On the third day, having covered only a few kilometres, the expedition very nearly came to an abrupt end as a crocodile decided that the inflatable canoe was a possible meal. The two boats were floating gently down the river, and Sean was leaning back to avoid the low-hanging tree branches, when he was alerted by a loud swirl in the water ahead of him. Thinking it may be a fish or some other water animal, he raised his head to look at the disturbance.

At that instant, a crocodile of mean proportions took the rear of the inflatable in its jaws and focused its small, beady eyes on Sean. 'This was exactly where my head had been resting and the snout was literally centimetres from my hand. I could have put my fingers up its nostrils without any trouble!' recalled Sean. For a moment or two the croc savoured the canoe and then closed its jaws. Perhaps it was the sudden rush of air or Sean's angry outburst that persuaded the crocodile to let go, but Sean was greatly relieved when it opened its mouth, backed off and disappeared under the water.

The craft was badly damaged but repairs were done and the journey continued.

'For the next two or three days, we were constantly harassed by crocodiles, but none came as close as the first one. Some bumped the canoes with their snouts, and their scaly backs could be felt through the seat of our pants as they swam underneath the canoes.'

They paddled through a landscape dominated by water, a low horizon and very few people, which gave rise to feelings of loneliness and aloneness. 'The current was hardly discernible,' noted Sean and most of the time it was hard work paddling the inflatables, designed for white water rapids, down an almost motionless expanse of water. Sean lived mostly on fish he had caught, particularly barbel, but Carey was a vegetarian and she supplemented the fresh maize, melons and few vegetables they could barter with energy bars she had taken along with her.

A couple of days before they reached Mapai, Carey picked up a stomach bug from the inadequately purified water they were drinking. This, combined with the effects of the sun, a meagre diet and hard paddling made her really sick. Sean gave her antibiotics, only to discover that she was allergic to them, which made her feel even worse.

At Mapai they took a short break to walk to the village on the left bank. They photographed relics of the armed struggle and the devastation of the guerrilla camps by both Rhodesian and South African bombers.

The stretch between Mapai and the confluence of the Limpopo and Olifants rivers became a nightmare as Carey's physical state deteriorated and she lapsed increasingly into periods of unconsciousness and high fever. Sean had to wrap her in wet sheets, lay her in the bottom of the second canoe and tow her against an ever-increasing wind that was starting to blow directly up the river.

As they neared the Limpopo–Olifants confluence, the river broadened into a wetland covered from bank to bank with tall, tough reeds. Finding dry land at night became extremely difficult, and Sean recalled how he had to sit up in the bow of his canoe and cut a path through the reeds with a panga until they reached some suitable area where they could turn the inflatables upside down and use them as beds for the night.

At times they followed what looked like hippo paths through the reeds but not one single hippo was seen or heard during the entire trip. In fact, while they saw lots of birds and crocodiles, they saw no game animals at all, and very few cattle.

A day or so beyond the confluence, and approximately 40 kilometres before reaching the barrage at Macarretane, Sean realised that Carey was in no fit state to continue. He abandoned the canoes, cameras and all equipment and struggled 18 kilometres eastwards away from the river heading for the main road. He had to support and sometimes carry Carey as she was, by now, in a really bad way. At a small village called Mpelani they were cared for by the villagers, particularly a wonderful man called Amando (surname unknown), who spoke good English. They ceremoniously slaughtered a chicken, treated Carey with key parts, and made a delicious stew with the rest. Carey and Sean were given a hut, and their clothes washed and pressed.

For two weeks, they received the utmost care and attention from the villagers. A group of women went to the river and brought back the two canoes and all the equipment so hastily abandoned. Nothing was missing. 'Those weeks rearranged my whole view on Africa,' says Sean. 'I have never been treated so kindly and so generously in all my life, and especially by people who lived such simple lives and who had really never had much contact with white people or the outside world before. We formed a friendship and bond that I still try and maintain on my irregular trips back into Mozambique.'

Three weeks later Carey was well enough to continue the journey. At Macarretane they were met by a support team and provided with supplies. They found that the Macarretane barrage reduces the water flow quite considerably, so they drove downstream towards Chokwe looking for a place to get back onto the river.

Shortly before the town they found a spot, but both energy and enthusiasm were running low, especially as the headwinds became stronger and metre-high waves rolled up the river towards them. 'I guess we had both just had enough,' said Sean, 'and we decided one dark and rainy night to call it quits.'

And so the dream of reaching the sea came to an end, but Sean and Carey stayed on exploring villages and experiencing 'the incredible feeling of remoteness and isolation' one gets in a vast flat land so seemingly full of emptiness.

BELOW: Canoeists on the Ivory Trail take a break from paddling their sturdy Canadian-style canoes from Pont Drift to the river's junction with the Shashe River during the '70s and '80s.

ABOVE: Robert Perkins and Bonus Lunga.

Filmmaker Robert Perkins has canoed on many major rivers around the world, including the arctic wilderness of Russia's Kamchatka peninsula. However, he says that the most exotic journey he has undertaken was a trip down the Limpopo River in 2002.

I was looking for a positive story in the everyday life along a river for American and European audiences, to counter the hysteria following the World Trade Centre attacks on 11 September 2001. Stimulated by childhood memories of my father reading the Kipling's children's story about how the elephant got his trunk, I decided on the 'great grey-green, greasy Limpopo River, all set about with fever-trees', and spent eight weeks on the river with a young canoeist from Zimbabwe, Bonus Lunga.

'We canoed in the headwaters, but much of the river was just too low that year. From the Crocodile–Marico confluence onwards we paddled most of the river, leaving out the rocky stretches below Mabalel and Limpopo Gorge below Malala Drift. We had a shore crew that struggled to link up with us and we were on our own for long stretches.

'Bonus and I travelled as explorers through the varied terrain the river has to offer: people's backyards, townships, small villages, resorts, game reserves and national parks, and finally arrived at the Indian Ocean south of Xai-Xai in Mozambique. It was tough going at times: in the early stages the water was too shallow, we were threatened by suspicious border guards (they were holding elections that spring in Zimbabwe), suffered infectious tick bites, and dodged hippos and crocs along the northern edge of Kruger Park. But in equal measure wonderful people freely gave us guidance, water and food when we needed it.

'One magical evening towards the end of the trip we made camp on a point near a mangrove swamp. When the tide went out, it revealed thick black mud, along with huge armies of small blue crabs. We set up our tents and gathered wood for our fire. We could hear the sound of surf breaking far in the distance, but were tired after the long trip together and eager to reach the ocean, which Bonus had never seen. Soon stars were thick above us and in the surge of the river-tide below us appeared bright phosphorous as schools of fish swam by or the small wind waves broke against the mud. We cooked our meal of rice and meat by firelight surrounded by the dark and silence of the river.

'As we sat by the fire I heard the sound of rubber boots with water in them approaching. At the edge of our fire's light appeared a man so black that I could see only his yellow rain jacket standing in the firelight as though it held no body. Across his left shoulder was draped a fishing net with small lead weights along its bottom. We beckoned him to join us. He squatted and with hand signals and some common words, Bonus and I learned that he fished at night walking the bank of the Limpopo listening for rising fish. On hearing them he'd throw his net. He complained that since the recent flood that straightened the river's course the fishing was not as good. He was glad to eat our leftover rice and meat. We talked for a while but mostly we just sat in silence, listening to the pop and crackle of the wood burning. At times the wind carried the sound of women singing from miles away. It was like no other evening in my life: just three men sitting silently by the fire beside the Limpopo River, under the starry African night sky.

'Saluting good-bye, but without saying anything, the fisherman got up and walked away from the fire blending again into the night, the sound of his rubber boots growing fainter and fainter after his yellow jacket disappeared from the light of the fire …'

FOLLOWING SPREAD: A young boy paddles in the clear, shallow waters of the Limpopo alongside the Zimbabwean bank of Sentinel Ranch.

Limpopo Journey
– The Source

'Our next movement brought us to the source of the Oori or Limpopo … Fed by many streams from the Cashan range.'
– WILLIAM CORNWALLIS HARRIS

The Headwaters of the Limpopo

What is the source of a river, especially when that river has spread its fingers over a huge part of the South African landscape? One definition could be 'the highest point at the furthest end of the longest branch', which would probably take us to a trickle of rainwater down one of the concrete sides of the Hillbrow Tower! Some people have even tried to 'hijack' it – a group has suggested renaming the Braamfonteinspruit as the Limpopo River, and a church in Parktown, Johannesburg was even renamed 'St Mary on the Limpopo' in 1982.

Clearly the source is the great divide of the Highveld, the watershed that runs through the middle of Johannesburg, called the Witwatersrand. By its very nature, the water running off a watershed consists of lots and lots of little trickles, which gradually come together to form a stream, and many streams come together to form a river. So which trickle or stream do we start with?

After lengthy and interesting discussions on the matter, we have used our authors' prerogative to decide that, while sites should clearly be close to the furthest ends of the river, we will not be dictated to by cold geographical facts; the source or sources we choose should also have interest, significance and a 'sense of place'. Following this approach, we have selected four starting points for our journey down the Limpopo River:

- The spectacular Witpoortjie Waterfall in the Walter Sisulu National Botanical Gardens is the furthest feature in the **Crocodile River**, and has for long been claimed as the source of the Limpopo.
- Constitution Hill right on the watershed and flowing into the **Braamfonteinspruit** has great significance for this country, because many famous political prisoners were imprisoned there, and the Constitutional Court is the custodian of our world-renowned Constitution.
- The most southerly tributary of the Crocodile is the **Jukskei River** which starts close to the centre of Johannesburg, the bustling city built on the fabulous wealth of the richest gold reef in the world. Right near the top end of the Jukskei is the Ellis Park Sports Precinct, housing rugby, football, athletics, tennis and swimming in three major stadiums for a sports-mad South Africa.
- The beginning of the **Pienaars River** at Spitskop in the Bronberg south-east of Pretoria is reputed to be the furthest point that a drop of water would have to travel to get to the Limpopo River Mouth (presently unconfirmed as 1 750 kilometres). The Bronberg is a well-known biodiversity 'hotspot' on the Highveld.

OPPOSITE: The Witpoortjie Waterfall near the source of the Crocodile River is located in the Walter Sisulu Botanical Gardens, a favourite recreational area dating back to the late 1800s.

PREVIOUS SPREAD: Agriculture (irrigation) accounts for 62% of all surface water used in South Africa, followed by domestic and municipal use at 27%. (Source: WNC, Water Symposuim, August 2015.)

A fifth candidate is the 'eye' of the Marico River since, in the white man's terminology, the Limpopo River itself only starts when the Crocodile and Marico rivers come together at Olifants Drift.

The Crocodile River at the National Botanical Gardens

The Witpoortjie Waterfall has been used as a recreational site since the late 1800s. It seems that it got its name from the fact that visitors travelling by train from Johannesburg would arrive at Witpoortjie Station and then walk down to the falls. In fact, the furthest point of the Crocodile is close to the Witpoortjie Station, about three kilometres upstream from the falls. These attractive falls, in a national botanical garden, seem to be an appropriate place to start our Limpopo journey.

The area around the falls was only developed as a national botanical garden in 1982, and was named after Walter Sisulu, the renowned African National Congress leader, in 2004. The gardens have good examples of the geology of these quarzitic ridges, a cycad garden, a water garden, dam and wetland, and great hiking trails. Apart from the falls, its other well-known feature is the only pair of nesting Verreauxs' eagles (black eagles) in urban Johannesburg.

Northwards from the Walter Sisulu National Botanical Gardens the river travels through suburbs and smallholdings on relatively flat landscape based on ancient, three-billion-year-old rocks. Here it has to contend with the usual problems of invasive plants, littering, pollution and soil erosion, until it suddenly hits the far more recent dolomites, which provided the limestone conditions suitable for fossil formation in the Cradle of Humankind World Heritage Site. The Crocodile travels up the side of 'the Cradle', but an important tributary, the Blaauwbankspruit, flows right between the most important fossil sites (see page 61).

North of Johannesburg are several east–west ridges, such as the Skurweberg, the Witwatersberg and the Magaliesberg, which block the northward flow of the Crocodile and other tributaries. The river then has to flow east or west along the ridge until it finds a passage through. As these poorts are relatively scarce, the rivers have to join together and share them. So the confluence of each tributary is always at the base of a ridge before squeezing through the poort.

OPPOSITE TOP: Constitution Hill is located on top of the watershed that flows into the Braamfonteinspruit. It has great significance for South Africa and is today the site of the Constitutional Court.

OPPOSITE BOTTOM: The Hartbeespoort Dam (completed in 1923) holds the waters of the Crocodile River and various tributaries at the entrance to a deep gorge in the Magaliesberg range.

Just east of the Cradle is the site where PJ Marais found traces of gold in the Crocodile and Jukskei rivers in 1853. He panned upstream to the confluence with the Braamfonteinspruit and then further up that river into Sandton, and found gold in all these headwaters of the Limpopo. Unfortunately for him he came close to, but never found, the richest gold deposit in the world, the Witwatersrand Reefs, just a few kilometres further on. He didn't even find the Black Reef, literally a few metres from where he panned the first gold in the Transvaal. There are historic mines at Tweefontein and Minnaar's Mine near Kromdraai in the Cradle of Humankind. The old Blaauwbank Mine, which is now a tourist attraction, is just west of Magaliesberg town.

After the Cradle of Humankind, the Crocodile is joined by first the Jukskei and then the Hennops River from Pretoria. It then flows through deep gorges through the Skurweberg and Witwatersberg ranges, before entering Hartbeespoort Dam near Broederstroom.

Constitution Hill and the Braamfonteinspruit

This leg of the journey starts at the furthest end of the Braamfonteinspruit on Constitution Hill,[1] which bore witness to the misery of the Johannesburg Prison, but blossomed after 1994 to be the seat of our world-famous Constitutional Court.

In 1892 Paul Kruger, the President of the South African Republic, approved the building of the first high-security prison on a hill overlooking central Johannesburg. From the beginning it served a dual purpose, since it was deliberately built on a hill from which the Boers could fire on any uprising from the pro-British *Uitlanders*. After the infamous Jameson Raid, the Fort with ramparts was added to the prison. The ramparts themselves provide the watershed, since a drop of water on the northern side would eventually find its way into the Limpopo River and on to the Indian Ocean, while a drop of water on the southern side would go into the Vaal and Orange system, and eventually end up in the Atlantic Ocean.

From the South African Great War onwards the 'guest list' in the prison is a veritable 'who's who' of resistance and struggle politics in the twentieth century (see box opposite).

An underground tunnel connects the Prison Complex with the old magistrate's court. It contains a double tunnel so that it could be racially segregated, with white prisoners travelling through one side, and black prisoners through the other.

The Old Fort Prison Complex was declared a national monument in 1964, and for many years was a symbol of Afrikaner nationalism. The prison was eventually closed in 1983.

Famous prisoners held in the Old Fort Prison Complex, commonly known as 'Number Four', on what is now Constitution Hill.[2]

- During the Anglo-Boer War the prison was quickly taken over by the British, and **pro-Boer sympathisers** were held there; four of them were the only people ever executed there (by firing squad).
- **Winston Churchill** was briefly held at the Old Fort during the Anglo-Boer War. Some other 'guests' of the Prison were more notorious gangsters and murderers.
- In 1900–03 legendary gangster **Nongoloza Mathebula** of the Ninevites Gang was imprisoned there. The Ninevites inspired the notorious 28s prison gang, still operational today.
- **Mahatma Gandhi** was imprisoned four times during the Passive Resistance Movement (1906, 1907, 1913, 1922).
- **Labour party leaders** were imprisoned during the 1913–14 strikes.
- **Boer General Christiaan de Wet** spent time there during the 1914 Rebellion against South Africa joining the war against Germany.
- **Daisy de Melker**, who murdered two husbands and a son in the late 1920s, was also imprisoned there.

- **White mineworkers** were imprisoned during the 1922 strike.
- **Ossewabrandwag leaders** were held there during World War II.
- Members of the **1955 Defiance Campaign** were imprisoned.
- Treason trialists were imprisoned, including **Nelson Mandela, Albert Luthuli, Joe Slovo, ZK Mathews, Walter Sisulu, Oliver Tambo, Helen Joseph, Moses Kotane, Lilian Ngoyi** and **Ruth First.**
- **Albertina Sisulu** and **Winnie Madikizela-Mandela** were imprisoned during the 1958 Pass Protests.
- **Robert Sobukwe** and other campaigners were held there during the Anti-Pass Campaign.
- Hundreds of activists were imprisoned during the State of Emergency after the 1960 Sharpeville Massacre.
- **Ellen Kuzwayo, Fatima Meer, Joyce Seroke** and **Winnie Madikizela-Mandela** were imprisoned during the 1976 Soweto Uprising.

After the formation of the Constitutional Court in 1994, the appointed justices looked for a permanent site and chose the Prison Complex partly because of its accessibility and space, but primarily because of its historical and symbolic importance. An international competition to design the new building was won by a group of South African architects, and it was opened on Human Rights Day, 21 March, in 2004.

From this lofty and symbolic ridge on the watershed above the Johannesburg city centre, water trickles down to what was the beginning of the Braamfonteinspruit. Nowadays the upper reaches are mostly concreted into storm-water drains.

Some years ago a small chapel of the St Mary's Cathedral in downtown Johannesburg was experiencing problems with damp. They discovered that it was situated on top of a spring, which is one of the extremities of the Braamfonteinspruit. Enquiries at Wits University suggested that this is the most southerly origin of the Limpopo River (actually it is not – the Jukskei is further south), and on the basis of this the Chapel was called St Mary on the Limpopo.[3]

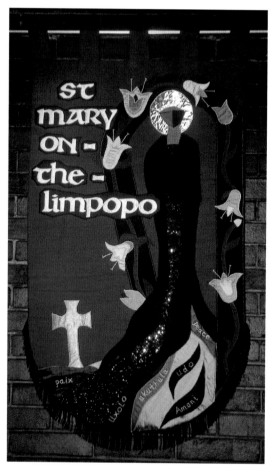

From where it turns northwards near the Johannesburg Country Club, the Braamfonteinspruit is a delightful green belt that provides recreation for thousands of residents. Some of it flows through private property, such as the exclusive Parkview Golf Course, but substantial stretches are open. A Braamfonteinspruit Trail was laid out some 25 years ago, and some of us joined other families in a delightful mountain bike ride alongside the Spruit in the Parkhurst, Delta Park and Craighall Park section. Although the belt is spoiled a bit by power lines, the river is clean and unpolluted, with attractive small dams and rapids. It continues past the Old Parktonian Association Sports Club and the suburb River Club and meanders through Bryanston and Rivonia to where it joins up with the Jukskei just north of Sunninghill.

The Jukskei River

The Jukskei River makes a wide arc around the end of Linksfield Ridge, and actually drains the southern slopes of the main Witwatersrand Ridge. It is therefore the most southerly of all the Limpopo's headwaters. Its highest point would be on the ridge itself, but the main fountain rises in the vicinity of the old Ellis Park stadium in the suburb of Doornfontein.

Ellis Park has been the home of rugby in Johannesburg since the first stadium was built on a quarry and garbage dump in 1927. The old stadium hosted over 90 000 spectators for some matches, and was a favoured test match venue. In 1980 the old stadium was demolished and replaced by a new, modern one that can accommodate 60 000 spectators.

Doornfontein was the original suburb of choice for the 'Randlords' – the mining magnates who made fortunes from the development of the gold mines nearby to become the economic engine of southern Africa – before they moved over the hill

BELOW: The Jukskei River passes through the large, eastern township of Alexandra that becomes littered, polluted and can be dangerous to citizens in times of flood.

OPPOSITE: St Mary on the Limpopo, a small chapel of St Mary's Cathedral in Parktown, was found to straddle a spring and so it was named thus in 1982.

to the Parktown ridge. A number of stately early homes are still preserved, mostly by private owners, and some years ago were linked together in a Randlords Heritage Walk as part of the Jukskei Trail.

From the thriving sports complex and the elegant homes of the old days, the Jukskei plummets in prestige, and becomes nothing more than a littered, polluted storm-water drain, that is often buried underground! Its only redeeming factor is that the sides of the canal were laboriously built with rather attractive stonework.

For the first few kilometres, the canalised stream travels generally eastwards through what are now the industrial and low-income suburbs of Lorentzville, Judith's Paarl and Bezuidenhout Valley (Bez Valley), with the occasional park and playground for the local children. In Bezuidenhout Park the canal stops. It is joined by other streams, and soon it opens out into the Bruma Lake Complex.

From here it flows through a green belt, around the end of Linksfield Ridge next to the N3 highway, through Alexandra township, where it becomes littered and polluted again, and continues north to the Sunninghill area where it is joined by the Sand Spruit and the Braamfontein Spruit. Twenty kilometres later it joins the Crocodile north of Lanseria airport at the Renosterfontein Conservancy.

The Pienaars River and the Bronberg

The longest tributary of the Limpopo River starts at the Bronberg, on the outskirts of Pretoria, and flows northwards as the Pienaars River. The Bronberg is one of a small number of quartzite ridges of Gauteng that are still in a relatively well-conserved state, and have a unique plant species composition that occurs nowhere else. It is considered to be a Biodiversity Hotspot and harbours a number of Red Data mammals, including substantial populations of one of the rarest South African mammals, Juliana's golden mole, as well as six species of rare reptiles and a rare rock scorpion. Endangered plants include an oleander, an orchid and a lily, with a number of other species considered 'rare'.

From the Bronberg the Pienaars River flows northwards to Roodeplaat Dam, an important recreation area for Pretoria, and on up the western side of the ambitious Dinokeng Nature Reserve that is presently being established on the boundary between Gauteng and Limpopo provinces. North of Hammanskraal it turns westwards, into Klipvoor Dam in the Borakalalo Game Reserve, and then joins the Crocodile at Buffelspoort. It is this long arc into the edge of the Springbok Flats that increases the distance of the Bronberg from the sea, and makes the Pienaars River the longest tributary of the Limpopo.

Cradle of Humankind World Heritage Site

The Cradle of Humankind World Heritage Site has yielded far more hominid fossils than any other site in the world. It was one of the first World Heritage Site listings for South Africa in 1999. The dolomite limestone rock formation provides ideal conditions for the formation of rock-hard breccia fossils. There are many fossil sites in the 47 000 hectares of the proclaimed area, and almost certainly there are some that have not yet been discovered. For the World Heritage Site Nomination, 13 of the key fossil sites were specified. They all have a range of animal species, from ancient baboons and monkeys to sabre-toothed cats, giant hyenas, three-toed horses, giant hyrax, short-necked giraffe, giant buffalo with horns three metres from tip to tip and a host of smaller animals. As the nomination document[4] says:

'These sites are valuable for the study of extinctions of communities of animals and the conditions under which the ancient faunae of Africa have either adapted or become extinct. The cave deposits contain outstanding examples of ecological and biological processes in deep time ... a series of ecosystems, each frozen or fossilised at its moment in time.'

Of the 13 sites, seven have so far yielded hominid fossils. Sterkfontein has proved to be the most productive, with no less than 600 specimens of *Australopithecus africanus*, including 'Mrs Ples', and the almost complete skeleton known as 'Little Foot'. The most specimens of the slightly later *Paranthropus robustus* have been found at Swartkrans (over 300 specimens from at least 85 individuals) and at Drimolen (75 specimens).

Swartkrans has yielded the earliest evidence for the controlled use of fire, about a million years ago, and a range of stone and bone tools. Smaller numbers of early humans *Homo ergaster* have been found at each of these sites, and Gladysvale, Kromdraai, Coopers and Gondolin have produced a few hominids of the above species. These large numbers have allowed scientists to study whole populations of hominid ancestors, rather than just individuals, to link into the ecological information from other animal fossils.

On 13 September 2013, two South African 'cavers', Steven Tucker and Rick Hunter, made the most astonishing fossil discovery in a cave known as the Rising Star within the Cradle of Humankind, west of Johannesburg. This was subsequently named *Homo naledi* (in Sotho *naledi* means 'star'). For the full report, see *National Geographic*, October 2015, 'Almost Human'. Shreeve, J.

The Cradle of Humankind has a number of other interesting attractions as well. It is a great place to see stromatolites, evidence of the first forms of life on Earth. They were formed by layer upon layer of blue-green algae that grew more than two billion years ago in the oxygen-poor, carbon-dioxide-dominated atmosphere, depositing calcium and generating the oxygen essential to support life as we know it today. There are also caves with beautiful stalagmites and stalactites, of which the most accessible, and one of the most impressive, is Wonder Cave. Unfortunately many pristine caves were blasted out when the demand for lime in the goldfields was at its peak early last century!

The Cradle of Humankind World Heritage Site provides a range of activities to visitors, including fascinating displays at Sterkfontein Museum and the grand new Maropeng facility. At Sterkfontein tours are organised down into the caves, which gives a feeling of the limestone formations that created the conditions for fossils, and the flow of clear underground, lime-rich water that feeds into the Crocodile River.

It is important to realise that the early hominids, and the exotic animals that accompanied them, did not just occur in the Sterkfontein area. They would have occurred over most of southern Africa, but Sterkfontein had the right conditions to capture and preserve the fossils.

BELOW: Aerial pesticide 'crop-spraying' is another potential hazard for fresh-water eco systems.

FOLLOWING SPREAD: Bruma Lake created from the outflow of the waters from the Jukskei River and other small streams near the suburb of Kensington and Bedfordview.

The good-looking young army captain sat back on a rock, cradling his double-barrelled hunting rifle, and watched as his heavily laden ox wagons crested the pass at Commando Nek for the last time. The trip so far had been the experience of a lifetime, and he looked forward to showing off his collection of animals to the scientific community.

William Cornwallis Harris was stationed in Bombay and was sent to the Cape on leave in the 1800s, during which time he carried out a lengthy hunting trip by ox wagon into 'the territories of Chief Moselekatse'. After gleaning as much information as he could from Andrew Smith, David Hume and Robert Scoon he travelled to Kuruman, where Robert Moffat gave him a recommendation to Mzilikazi, who was now based north of Zeerust. His many exotic gifts pleased Mzilikazi, who gave him permission to hunt in the area of the 'Cashan Mountains' (the Magaliesberg), and provided guides.

In addition to being an enthusiastic hunter, Harris wanted to make a contribution to natural history, and collected at least two of every species of game that he could find, preserving the horns and skins, painting pictures of them in their natural habitat, and giving detailed descriptions of their habits. His most exciting encounter so far had been hunting giraffe by charging into the midst of a group, selecting one individual and galloping with it while firing shots at point-blank range.

The densities of game he recorded are almost unbelievable. For example, rhinoceros were so plentiful that 'on our way from the waggons [sic] to a hill, not half-a-mile distant, we counted no less than twenty two of the white species of rhinoceros, and were compelled in self-defence to slaughter four'. He even recounts killing rhinos for rations!

In spite of this excessive slaughter, he was not as bloodthirsty as some other hunters that followed him, and felt pangs of remorse such as when he shot a cow elephant and her tiny baby 'ran round its mother's corpse with touching demonstrations of grief, piping sorrowfully, and vainly attempting to raise her with its tiny trunk'.

Harris hunted mostly in the Magaliesberg area, but then did a rapid trip up to the Tropic of Capricorn, following up along the Crocodile to about 40 miles (64 kilometres) north of the confluence with the Marico, and he was therefore one of the first Englishmen to describe what is now known as the Limpopo River.

A few days after his return to the Magaliesberg Harris collected his most valuable specimen, a magnificent male sable antelope, which was previously unknown to science. After following it for three days, he eventually bagged it and describes his excitement as he examined it minutely, carefully sketched it and skinned it to send it back to the British Museum. For decades after this the sable was known as the 'Harris buck'.

Harris's collection of specimens and drawings were a sensation in Britain, and his books of the safari were the first ever devoted exclusively to game hunting in Africa. They give a vivid description of the huge herds of game that once roamed this part of the Limpopo River.

The Magaliesberg

The Magaliesberg has played an important role in the history of this part of South Africa, and it is crossed at right angles by the Crocodile River. With high cliffs on the southern side along most of its length it was a substantial barrier, with only a few poorts that could be traversed comfortably. Several of the early explorers travelled along it, either to the north or the south, and during the Anglo-Boer War it was used as a barrier by the British to try to trap the Boers.

Magaliesberg Proclaimed a World Biosphere Reserve by Unesco[6]

After nearly a decade of lobbying and sustained efforts by a small committee of dedicated environmentalists, the Magaliesberg was declared a World Biosphere Reserve on 9 June 2015.

The announcement was made in Paris by the International Coordinating Council of the Programme on Man and the Biosphere (MAB). This is a Unesco programme that aims to build a supportive and sustainable relationship between people and their environments. In effect, this means a specific focus on safeguarding natural ecosystems through innovative approaches to economic development.

The World Network of Biosphere Reserves, which Magaliesberg now joins, is composed of 631 biosphere reserves in 119 countries.

Vincent Carruthers, past chair of the Magaliesberg Biosphere Initiative Group (MBIG) and renowned author of *The Magaliesberg*, the most authoritative study of the mountain range, said that this announcement was the culmination of a campaign that began in 2006.

'I'm most grateful there is now international recognition of this great mountain range that has witnessed the whole span of life, from its very origins,' he said. 'The Magaliesberg is almost 100 times older than Mount Everest and half the age of the Earth, a unique treasure for us in this part of Africa.'

The Magaliesberg Biosphere Reserve covers almost 358 000 hectares – 58 000 making up the core area, 110 000 hectares the buffer area and 190 000 hectares the transition area.

Early Iron Age Occupation

Broederstroom, just upstream from the Hartbeespoort Dam next to the Crocodile River, is the oldest known Iron Age site in the inland areas of South Africa, dated from AD 350 onwards. Iron from surface deposits nearby was smelted in charcoal furnaces with bellows blowing air through clay pipes that brought them to the high heat needed. The iron was beaten into hoes, weapons and trade articles. As the first group to use iron, they are classed as Early Iron Age people. In about the seventh century AD they disappeared, possibly due to the onset of a colder, drier climate, and Stone Age hunter-gatherers prevailed again for the next 600 years.

Middle Iron Age cattle farmers came back to the area in about AD 1200 and lived in the foothills of the Magaliesberg and along the Crocodile River. They grew crops, mainly sorghum and millet, and had cylindrical huts with conical thatched roofs. Stone walls first appeared in about AD 1600, which identified the transition to what is called the Late Iron Age. They were early Tswana-speaking people and can be directly followed through oral history to modern Tswana people living in the area today. People often gathered together in large towns, and smelting of iron, copper and tin were key industries.

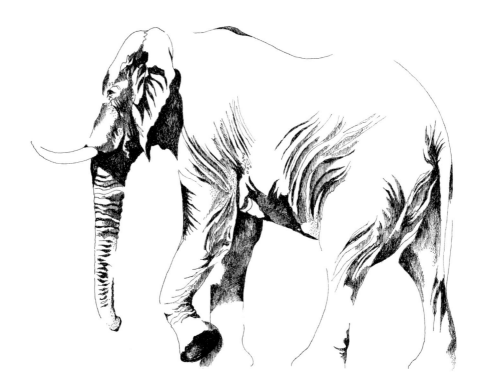

Tswana and Ndebele in the Early 1800s

The *Difecane* (or *Mfecane*; Zulu for 'The Crushing') was a period of great disruption among the people of the central southern African Highveld. Groups who had been displaced by Zulu expansionism and drought attacked their neighbours, who then attacked and stole from others. This ripple effect stretched right up to the Magaliesberg, and many villages were devastated.

Then in 1823 the warlike Pedi invaded, captured herds of cattle, and carried off women and children. This fate nearly befell young Mogale, heir to the Po Chiefdom. He was hidden by his grandparents, and returned later to play an important role in the mountains, which came to be named after him.

The Pedi invasion was followed by the invasion of Ndebele under Mzilikazi, a Zulu chief who defied Shaka and fled with some of his people. He swept northwards through Commando Nek and defeated the Kwena and other tribes, and ruthlessly absorbed them into his army. Initially he established his capital at Kungwini, north of Pretoria, and conquered the local Tswanas from there. However, Kungwini was destroyed by a Zulu reprisal raid in 1832, and Mzilikazi decided to move his capital more to the west, to Gabeni in the Marico basin. After several battles with the Voortrekkers who settled in the area in 1836, the Ndebele were driven far to the west to Mosega north of Zeerust. Eventually they were evicted from there and moved in stages up to Bulawayo in the future Zimbabwe.

Silkaatsnek is a pass just to the east of the Hartbeespoort gorge that was named after Mzilikazi because of his major centre Dinaneni on the northern slopes, close to where a pitched battle with the Zulus was fought.

Early Missionaries, Hunters, Traders and Naturalists

A wide range of missionaries, hunters, traders and naturalists visited this part of the Magaliesberg in the mid-1800s, and gave us an impression of what this stretch of the Crocodile River was like.

Some of the first were three Scotsmen from Grahamstown, McLuckie, Scoon and Hume, in the 1820s. They told Mzilikazi about the work of missionaries to the south, and Mzilikazi immediately despatched a deputation to Robert Moffat at Kuruman. They persuaded Moffat to accompany them to Mzilikazi's kraal at Kungwini, where he stayed for eight days. This was the beginning of a rather unlikely friendship between Moffat and Mzilikazi that smoothed the passage for many later visitors from the Cape. Travellers who had come via Kuruman were welcomed by the Ndebele because Moffat had approved of them; travellers from any other direction were treated with suspicion and were attacked. Moffat had moved along the northern foothills of the Magaliesberg, crossed the range at Commando Nek and the Crocodile River where the Hartbeespoort Dam is now.

Moffat facilitated the passage of the first scientific expedition, that of Dr Andrew Smith in 1835, which aimed to record the people and wildlife, both by collecting specimens and in paintings, for the South African Museum which he had recently founded. To this end no less than three artists accompanied the expedition, George Ford, Henry Lowe and Charles Bell, and these painters brought back a wonderful record of the landscapes, the animals and the people of this part of the Crocodile River. Smith travelled along the southern side of the Magaliesberg, crossed at Commando Nek, and then travelled up to Pilanesberg and on to the Limpopo.

Shortly after this the Indian army captain William Cornwallis Harris hunted in the Crocodile River area in 1836 (see box on page 63). Although primarily a hunting expedition, he also made a substantial contribution to science, by writing books and illustrating them with his own artwork.

ABOVE: Roualeyn Gordon-Cumming shot this white rhino during his 1846 hunting expedition in the Marico district. The horn measured 54 inches (1.37 metres) – this is the longest horn ever recorded. It was stolen a number of years ago from the family estate in Scotland and was never seen again! (Collection R Gordon-Cumming)

Smith's and Harris's accounts stimulated a number of hunting expeditions, many of which later went directly from Kuruman up to the Limpopo, because in the Magaliesberg area of the Crocodile the large game, particularly elephants, were rapidly hunted out after the arrival of the Voortrekkers and the expulsion of Mzilikazi. Nevertheless, the Crocodile was visited by a range of naturalists, missionaries and artists, who were to become celebrated in their fields, such as missionary and explorer David Livingstone (see box below), artist Thomas Baines, and naturalists Joseph Burke, Carl Zeyher, Johan Wahlberg and William Atherstone.

The Magaliesberg also served as a base for hunters who penetrated into the

David Livingstone, missionary explorer[8]

David Livingstone started off at Moffat's Mission in Kuruman, but in 1844 moved on and set up a mission with Rogers Edwards at Mabotsa, close to the Ngotwane tributary of the Limpopo, 50 kilometres north-west of Zeerust. There he was visited and befriended by William Cotton Oswell, a British hunter based in India, who thereafter became a benefactor of several of his exploration trips into Africa.

After he was mauled by a lion, Livingstone went back to Kuruman where he was nursed by, and then married, Robert Moffat's daughter Mary. The couple moved on to set up a new mission, Chonwane, also close to the Ngotwane, just to the west of present-day Madikwe Game Reserve. There he made what appears to be his only successful conversion to Christianity, the local Chief Sechele.

A year later Sechele and his people moved to Kolobeng, near Gaborone, due to problems with water, and Livingstone followed him. From this base, which was also close to the Ngotwane

River, he set out on his first trip with Oswell, to discover Lake Ngami.

Livingstone provided information and assistance to several hunters who visited the Limpopo River area, most notably Cumming, whose ox wagons were immobilised because all the oxen had died of *nagana* (a cattle disease transmitted by the tsetse fly).

In the mid-1840s he made a series of eastward treks across the Limpopo River into the Transvaal Republic, encountering as he did the Dutch frontier farmers. Livingstone's relationship with the local tribes made him a target of suspicion among the Dutch settlers, and he was called all sorts of names. He took this as a compliment, for it showed the blacks how committed he was to them!

These travels took Livingstone first into the Magaliesberg mountains and then again in 1847, together with his wife Mary, to Rustenburg and on up towards Potgietersrus – now Mokopane. These travels are described as 'apprenticeship hinterland. For example, well-known hunter Henry Hartley had a farm in the Magaliesberg and regularly went on hunting expeditions to the Limpopo and beyond, becoming a regular visitor and special confidant of Mzilikazi and later Lobengula. He also helped prospector Carl Mauch to find the Tati and other goldfields. Hartley was particularly interesting because he accomplished all this travelling with a club foot, as well as hunting on horseback.[7]

FOLLOWING SPREAD: The beauty and magic of the Limpopo in its many moods, sometimes violent, most times peaceful, and always captivating.

routes'. From an undated map they travelled from Potgietersrus westwards towards the Limpopo River utilising the abundance of the waters of the Mogalakwena, Palala and Mokolo rivers and numerous other streams arising within the Palala Plateau.

A National Heritage Monument marks a unique grove of ana trees (*Faidherbia albida*) that provided a comfortable place of rest with water nearby – in fact the Mogalakwena. The area is rather unique, since these trees occur nowhere else in the Waterberg. Ana trees are a spectacular feature along the north-eastern banks of the Limpopo River bordering Botswana, Zimbabwe and Mozambique. It is here in 1847 that Livingstone is reputed to have rested with his wife, followers and draft animals. This monument is situated some 15 kilometres from the present-day town of Mokopane.

The party once again connected with the Limpopo River following the north curve of the mountain range in a south-westerly direction,

for travel by wagon over the plateau would have proved arduous.

While Livingstone was away in 1852, his house at Kolobeng was ransacked by the Boers. A statement by General Smuts many years later in 1929 during an address in Edinburgh gives rich insights into the matter:

'I once took the opportunity to discuss the matter with President Kruger, and his explanation of the differences which arose between the Boers and Livingstone was that Gordon-Cumming – another of your errant countrymen – had supplied the border tribes with rifles and ammunition in exchange for ivory, and the Boers, finding the natives armed, concluded – erroneously – that Livingstone had done so, and treated him accordingly.'

Some people say that Livingstone was far too serious and intense, but he did have a lighter side. In a letter to his wife he wrote: 'We shall remove more easily now that we are lightened of our furniture'!

The South African Republic and the Anglo-Boer War

With the expulsion of Mzilikazi from the region in 1837, the area was rapidly settled by Voortrekkers. Every white male was allowed two farms of around 3 000 hectares each, and those who led commandos against the local population received land grants rather than cash. In this way Paul Kruger became an extensive landowner. The valleys south of the Magaliesberg and along the Crocodile were among the earliest to be settled.

The Trekkers soon pressed the local tribes into service, established water furrows and orchards and became quite settled with only the occasional excitement of a commando to punish local tribes who rebelled against their position of servitude. These independent-minded Trekkers refused to live under British law, and were granted independence by the Sand River Convention in 1852. However, the Convention itself sparked a serious confrontation between rival Boer leaders Potgieter and Pretorius, and bloodshed was only avoided at a reconciliation in Rustenburg later the same year. Later tensions built up again to the point where rival Boer armies of Van Rensburg on the one side, and Schoeman, Viljoen and Pretorius on the other confronted each other at the Crocodile River, just north of what is now Hartbeespoort Dam. Although this is sometimes called a 'Civil War', only one person was killed and several wounded before future president Marthinus Pretorius intervened and managed to stop the fighting. This is commemorated by a monument close to the tarred road just north of Silkaatsnek.

The Magaliesberg in the Crocodile River area became an important theatre of the Second Anglo-Boer War of 1899–1902. In June 1900, Lord Roberts occupied Pretoria, more than six months after the skirmishes in the Tuli area further downstream (outlined in box on page 102). However, it became clear that the Boers had not accepted defeat, and this phase marked their changeover to guerrilla tactics. The Magaliesberg was a useful barrier for the British to try to trap the Boer commandos. Lord Kitchener's 'scorched earth' policy cleared the 'blockhouse enclosures' and managed to net a substantial number of Boers during the rest of the war.

There were a few battles in the Magaliesberg in July and August 1900. Two engagements took place close to the Crocodile River, at Silkaatsnek, the pass through the Magaliesberg five kilometres to the east of the river, which is on the strategically important main road from Pretoria to Rustenburg. On 11 July of that

OPPOSITE: Captain William Cornwallis Harris, a wealthy English military officer and sportsman, conducted an expedition in the area of the Crocodile River in 1836.

year Colonel HR Roberts's battalion of the Lincoln Regiment was sent to Silkaatsnek to replace the Scot Grey's cavalry who were to join a force to relieve the pressure on Rustenburg. Roberts had lots of soldiers, but neglected to place guards on the high cliffs above the pass, which was occupied during the night by Boer General De la Rey's commando. The British were placed for an attack from the south, and found they could not train their guns high enough for the ridges above. The Boers were in a completely dominant position, and maintained such a withering fire that Roberts was forced to surrender in the evening. By then 72 of the 240 men had been killed or wounded. This was a major victory for the Boers, and helped boost their morale substantially.

Three weeks later the British retook Silkaatsnek with a large force. There was a fierce fight, during which a certain Private W House of the Royal Berkshire Regiment was awarded the Victoria Cross for bravery. The Boer commando retreated, managing to evade the force that had been sent to the north of the range to catch them in a pincer movement.

The Crocodile River crossing at Hartbeespoort was a critically important strategic position, and one of the largest British permanent supply camps was established at Rietfontein (now Ifafa on the Hartbeespoort Dam). The bridge and hills overlooking the river were extensively fortified and some of the old forts can still be seen today. The Rietfontein military cemetery can also be visited.

ABOVE: Elephant hunting for ivory in the 19th century wiped out the species and most of the large game right up to the Limpopo River and beyond by the turn of the century.

OPPOSITE: The Braamfonteinspruit is a much-loved green belt area used by thousands of outdoor enthusiasts.

Hartbeespoort Dam

The possibility of a major dam in the Crocodile River at Hartbeespoort was investigated in 1913, but construction was delayed. The first delay was caused by the rebellion against South Africa's invasion of 'German South West Africa' early in World War I, much of which was played out in the Magaliesberg area. The second delay was caused by major floods in 1918 which destroyed much of the work that had already been done. The dam was finally completed in 1923.

The construction of the Hartbeespoort Dam, as well as the other dams in the Magaliesberg area, played an important role in the creation of employment for white farmers who had been evicted by landowners during the post-war depression, both in the construction itself and in the work it created on the many irrigation farms downstream in the Crocodile River Valley.

The dam receives an annual average of 225 million cubic metres, and irrigates 130 square kilometres of farmland in the Brits district. In the early days it was also used to generate hydroelectric power, but now its main purposes are irrigation and recreation.

Recreational development around Hartbeespoort Dam has rocketed in the last decade, with a range of new housing developments, and three different yacht clubs using the dam, even though the water becomes so polluted during the summer that it is dangerous to swim in!

Conservation Areas and Recreation

With the burgeoning population of people in Johannesburg and Pretoria from the 1880s onward, and the increasing prosperity derived from a gold-based economy, the demand for recreation opportunities gradually increased. After World War II this demand exploded, and many landowners along the Crocodile River, and especially in the Magaliesberg, exploited their land by carrying out insensitive and unsustainable developments, such as sub-divisions for housing and allowing mass tourism that led to erosion and littering. This was compounded by government-driven infrastructure, such as radio masts, telephone masts, power lines, roads and quarries.

Luckily there was a core of landowners who valued the pristine quality of the area, and for several decades they managed to curb some of the more undesirable types of development.

Eventually, in 1977 the Magaliesberg was formally proclaimed the first 'nature area' in South Africa. After some misguided attempts by Nature Conservation to expropriate land from the very owners who had done so much to protect it in the interim, a more democratic Magaliesberg Protection Association was established. However, limited control has been exercised by the authorities over unscrupulous developers since, and the Magaliesberg remains under intense pressure.

Iron, Platinum and Irrigation

Below Hartbeespoort Dam the Crocodile River flows through the surface outcrop of the Bushveld Igneous Complex, with commercial activity dominated by irrigation farming using water from the Hartbeespoort Dam, platinum mining in the Rustenburg and Thabazimbi areas, and iron mining from Thabazimbi the 'Mountain of Iron'. Away from the river and the irrigation lands, most of the farms have been converted to hunting farms.

Further along the Crocodile, the Hartbeespoort Dam irrigation water is supplemented by the Rooikoppies, Vaalkop and Klipvoor dams, which are also used for recreation, especially fishing. The monotony of the flat terrain is occasionally broken by koppies or mountains such as the Langberg, Elandsberg, and the delightfully clumsy 'Swartwitpensbokfonteinberg' (the 'sable buck fountain mountain').

Shortly before Thabazimbi, the rich Merensky Reef of the Bushveld Igneous Complex curves round back towards the river, and Amandelbult Platinum Mine can be seen close by. As the river enters the mountains, it passes through the Vlieëpoort (Fly Pass), beyond which lay areas populated by the infamous tsetse fly in the mid-1800s. The Ben Alberts Nature Reserve lies on both sides of the river, and the Thabazimbi Mountain of Iron towers above.

Evidence has recently been found that iron ore was smelted by Iron Age people more than a thousand years ago, but there was little activity after that. The mountain was discovered by a European prospector in 1919, and mining only started by Iscor (Iron and Steel Corporation) in 1931. It is so rich that mining involves blasting and literally carrying the mountain away in huge ore-transporting trucks. The prosperity of the mine has turned Thabazimbi into a thriving mining town that is also the commercial centre for a large stretch of the Bushveld.

Thabazimbi has a mild tropical climate, but the early days were tough. Stories from the old days talk of tsetse fly, malaria (until 1941 the teachers received a 'fever allowance'), droughts (especially 1932/33, when zebras died in their hundreds), and floods of the Crocodile River.[9]

About 40 kilometres downstream from Thabazimbi, on the farm Gannahoek, is a large hollow baobab, the most southerly in this part of the country. In the old days up to seven hunters would climb through the hole and plug it with a thorn branch, to give protection from prowling wild animals. This area was also visited regularly by Paul Kruger on hunting expeditions in the 1860s.

At Olifants Drift the Crocodile joins the Marico, and from here on is called the Limpopo River.

BELOW: Kariba weed, beautiful but deadly to aquatic life in rivers, streams and dams.

OPPOSITE: Herman Charles Bosman's fictitious character, Oom Schalk Lourens, is portrayed here by the late actor Patrick Mynhardt in one of Bosman's famous stories.

The Marico River

The Eye of the Marico is a beautiful crystal-clear spring south of Zeerust that is popular with scuba divers. This wells up from the underground aquifers in the dolomitic rock that is prevalent in this region, and pumps an estimated 400 litres per second (or 1.4 million litres per hour) into the Marico River throughout the year.

The Marico would have remained a little-known, sleepy backwater of the Bushveld if it wasn't for Herman Charles Bosman. He was an Afrikaner who spent only six months in 1926 as a schoolteacher in the shadow of Abjaterskop in the Marico, but in that time the romance of the Bushveld captivated him, and he picked up a host of stories about the people living a hard, but simple, farming life in that part of the world. He presented these stories, in English, in such a rich and affectionate way that he developed a large following among English-speaking South Africans, and has become one of the best-known and most popular writers in the country. His life was filled with tragedy after he shot his stepbrother during a violent argument. After being condemned to death he was eventually reprieved, and spent four-and-a-half years in prison. He started writing his stories in prison, and continued overseas, dying at the young age of 46 in Lombardy East, within a kilometre of the Jukskei River. Since the 1960s thousands of people, especially in Johannesburg, have enjoyed an evening with the late actor Patrick Mynhardt telling Bosman stories as his fictitious character Oom Schalk Lourens in his *A Sip of Jerepigo, A Cask of Jerepigo, More Jerepigo* and others.

An important site bordering on the Marico is the Madikwe Game Reserve, which was developed as a major new game reserve by the progressive Bophuthatswana Parks Board in the 1990s. An area of 62 000 hectares was consolidated, and large numbers of game, including all of the Big 5, were reintroduced in the biggest translocation project in Africa. More than 20 upmarket safari lodges have been concessioned out, and the reserve has rapidly become one of the prime wildlife destinations in the country. It is also linked to the Pilanesberg through an ambitious Heritage Park, which adds yet more lodges to the total.

Just to the west of Madikwe is Abjaterskop, the small koppie lovingly described by Herman Charles Bosman, and a little further on the old mission station of Chonwane, established by David Livingstone in 1845.

As the Marico reaches the Botswana border it passes Derdepoort, the site of the infamous battle early in the Anglo-Boer War in November 1899,[10] a few weeks after the Tuli engagements (see page 98 in Chapter 3). The battle started off respectably, as an attack by about 100 troops of the Rhodesian Frontier Force on a Boer laager of about 80 strong. However, things went awry when the British commanding officer, Colonel Holdsworth, allowed about 700 armed Bakgatla warriors under Chief Linchwe to become involved. Both the Boers and the British had tried to keep the black tribes out of the 'White Man's War', but Colonel Holdsworth disobeyed orders and allowed them to cross the border from Botswana and join in the attack.

Headwaters timeline   *Note: MYA = Million Years Ago*

3.1–2.1 MYA	1.9–1.0 MYA	1.7–1.0 MYA	±1 MYA
Cradle of Humankind (COH) area inhabited by *Australopithecus africanus*.	COH inhabited by *Paranthropus robustus*.	COH inhabited by *Homo ergaster*.	Evidence for first controlled use of fire at Swartkrans.

1820s	1827	1835	1836
Difecane (Mfecane) period sees major disruption of local tribes in the Magaliesberg area.	Mzilikazi sweeps north, conquers the local Tswana groups such as Kwena, Po and Fokeng, and establishes his capital at Kungwini, north of Pretoria.	Dr Andrew Smith's trip to the Magaliesberg.	Arrival of the Voortrekkers; Cornwallis Harris's hunting trip to the Magaliesberg.

1853	1864	1886	1893
PJ Marais finds specks of gold in the Crocodile and Jukskei rivers.	Major confrontation at the Crocodile River just north of Hartbeespoort Dam ends the civil war between the Boer factions.	The Main Reef of the Witwatersrand is discovered, precipitating the main gold rush.	Johannesburg Prison officially opens on what was to become Constitution Hill.

1931	1936	1938	1947	1982
Iscor mine opens at Thabazimbi.	Broom finds an adult *Australopithecus africanus* at Sterkfontein, confirming Dart's interpretation of the Taung skull.	Broom finds first *Paranthropus robustus* fossil at Kromdraai.	Broom and Robinson find a complete *Australopithecus* skull, nicknamed 'Mrs Ples', at Sterkfontein.	Witwatersrand National Botanical Garden (later the Walter Sisulu National Botanical Gardens) opens, including Witpoortjie Waterfall.

The Bakgatla had an old score to settle from the days when Paul Kruger himself had publicly thrashed Linchwe's father, and they got a bit carried away. Holdsworth had withdrawn with his forces, which was seen as dishonourable by Linchwe, and the Bakgatla followed up the attack with raids on Boer farms and transport wagons almost as far as Pretoria. The Boers bitterly refer to the incident as the 'Murder of Derdepoort' and at least 30 Boers, including two women, were killed by the Bakgatla on that day and in a subsequent attack on a Boer transport wagon in February 1900.

From Derdepoort the Marico is the border with Botswana all the way to where it joins the Crocodile at Olifants Drift.

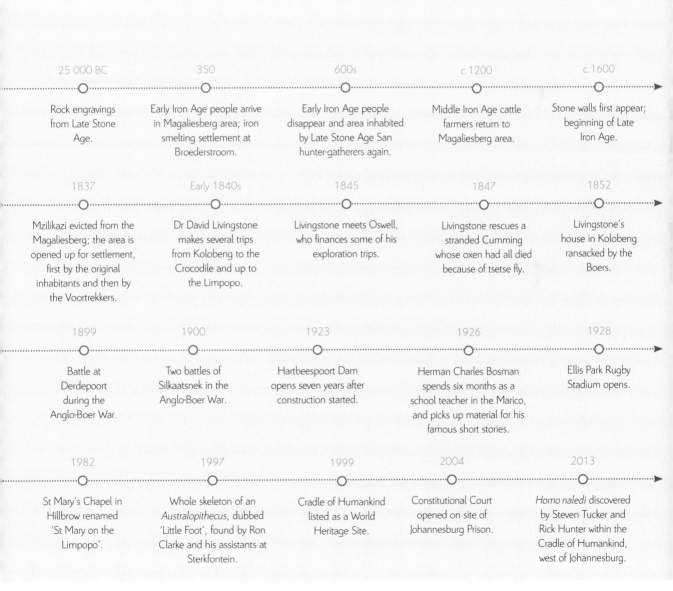

25 000 BC — Rock engravings from Late Stone Age.

350 — Early Iron Age people arrive in Magaliesberg area; iron smelting settlement at Broederstroom.

600s — Early Iron Age people disappear and area inhabited by Late Stone Age San hunter-gatherers again.

c.1200 — Middle Iron Age cattle farmers return to Magaliesberg area.

c.1600 — Stone walls first appear; beginning of Late Iron Age.

1837 — Mzilikazi evicted from the Magaliesberg; the area is opened up for settlement, first by the original inhabitants and then by the Voortrekkers.

Early 1840s — Dr David Livingstone makes several trips from Kolobeng to the Crocodile and up to the Limpopo.

1845 — Livingstone meets Oswell, who finances some of his exploration trips.

1847 — Livingstone rescues a stranded Cumming whose oxen had all died because of tsetse fly.

1852 — Livingstone's house in Kolobeng ransacked by the Boers.

1899 — Battle at Derdepoort during the Anglo-Boer War.

1900 — Two battles of Silkaatsnek in the Anglo-Boer War.

1923 — Hartbeespoort Dam opens seven years after construction started.

1926 — Herman Charles Bosman spends six months as a school teacher in the Marico, and picks up material for his famous short stories.

1928 — Ellis Park Rugby Stadium opens.

1982 — St Mary's Chapel in Hillbrow renamed 'St Mary on the Limpopo'.

1997 — Whole skeleton of an *Australopithecus*, dubbed 'Little Foot', found by Ron Clarke and his assistants at Sterkfontein.

1999 — Cradle of Humankind listed as a World Heritage Site.

2004 — Constitutional Court opened on site of Johannesburg Prison.

2013 — *Homo naledi* discovered by Steven Tucker and Rick Hunter within the Cradle of Humankind, west of Johannesburg.

CHAPTER 3

Olifants Drift
to Tuli

'The Limpopo normally is a sulky,
erratic river, full of sudden violence,
wearing itself out in mighty floods and
then relapsing from rage to a sullen
brooding in the captivity of its banks.'

– TV BULPIN

The Start of the Journey

From the confluence of the Crocodile and the Marico the Limpopo continues northwards through relatively flat country for some distance up to the border post of Zanzibar where one begins to encounter beautiful boulder granite outcrops dotted with baobab trees and some of the finest riverine forest along any stretch of the entire river. The riverbed is largely comprised of rocks and boulders, and has the steepest drop-off along the entire river's length. The beauty of the Limpopo is its constantly changing character. From the (wide) Motloutse River to the confluence of the Shashe and Limpopo, the river banks are steep with a sandy bed. In Jeppe's map of 1879 the river is spelt *Macloutsi*, yet another example of the mispronunciation of an African name.

Ngotwane River

The first major river after the Crocodile–Marico confluence is the Ngotwane, which enters from Botswana. It actually originates in South Africa some 220 kilometres to the south, near David Livingstone's original mission at Chonwane, and then goes into Botswana and via Lobatse and Gaborone to the Limpopo, passing his main mission station at Kolobeng. Cumming went via Kolobeng and followed the Ngotwane to the Limpopo, and Livingstone helped him out with spans of oxen from Kolobeng, when his had all died from tsetse fly.

Matlabas River

Shortly after the Ngotwane, the Matlabas joins from the South African side. This is the first of the four major rivers draining the Waterberg, which is also sometimes referred to as the Limpopo Highlands. Matlabas means the 'River of Sand' in Setswana, and the river rises high in the western rampart of the Waterberg's Marakele. From there it flows northwards through the relatively recently created Marakele National Park, a core part of the internationally recognised Waterberg Biosphere Reserve.

Willem van Riet mentions that there are lots of weirs in this stretch of the Limpopo River that keep standing water, to be used for irrigation (see box on page 38).

OPPOSITE: This massive 'sandstone' outcrop is known as Eagle's Rock and is located on the south bank of the Motloutse River, a Botswana tributary of the Limpopo.

PREVIOUS SPREAD: The Shashe River once drained the Okavango and Upper Zambezi rivers many millions of years ago before retreating and following its present-day route via the Victoria Falls (see Chapter 2.) Over 500 metres wide, it is an impressive sight during heavy rainfall.

Mokolo River

At the Mokolo River, Van Riet mentions that the character of the river changes; the banks are still forested, but every now and again a rock sticks out above the water and sand.

The name Mokolo means 'the surge', which indicates the propensity of this river to floods. It arises in the higher southern portion of the Waterberg to the east of the town Vaalwater and flows north-west through the Palala Plateau. The very last elephants in this part of South Africa were shot at Hermanusdorings in this catchment in 1924.

Palala River

Near the confluence with the Palala River (also known as the Lephalala), Van Riet had his first encounter with hippo in the Limpopo. The last hippo in the Palala, a lone bull, had been shot in the late 1950s. In 1985 Clive Walker, co-founder of Lapalala Wilderness, obtained three hippo from St Lucia in Zululand that were successfully re-introduced to the river. These were supplemented by a further five zoo-bred animals from the USA, and today hippos can be seen over large sections of the river.

Lapalala Wilderness was the first private conservation area in the Waterberg. Starting with 5 000 hectares in 1981, neighbouring properties were gradually added, and it is now stands at 42 000 hectares in size. Under Dale Parker and Clive's direction, it became a leader in private conservation, and was the first private operation to re-introduce black rhino in South Africa. It became a world leader in environmental education, with a focus on the Palala River, of which it protects some 80 kilometres on both banks and has now become a core area of the internationally recognised Waterberg Biosphere, which covers a massive 14 500 square kilometres. Today the property is co-owned by Dale Parker's son Duncan together with neighbour Gianni Ravassotti and continues with that legacy.

A key element in the conservation of this region and upon which the building blocks were laid in the formation of the Biosphere is the Waterberg Conservancy, an organisation of dedicated, passionate landowners who lead the continued restoration and awareness of 'wild country'.

The Waterberg can best be described as a giant wetland which, apart from the rivers mentioned above and the Mogalakwena River and the numerous small streams, represents a vital catchment area for the Limpopo River basin. The transformation from largely cattle and crop farming by the private sector over the past three decades has contributed enormously to the preservation of quality water emanating from these mountains and is unprecedented in South Africa. All the main Waterberg rivers contain naturally resident crocodile. The African rock python is common in the Waterberg and frequents the rivers.

Lotsane River

Just before Mmabolela the Lotsane River enters from the Botswana side. Close to the confluence are the Lotsane Ruins, which have intricate walling still intact, showing its Khami origin. Lotsane probably dates from AD 1400–1450, soon after the break up of Great Zimbabwe, and is thought to be the dynasty of a petty chief with a settlement that would have housed some 300–500 people.

The Lotsane River is also important in that in its upper reaches there are several hundred sites from a major cattle-herding culture that developed for a long period from about AD 700–1250.[1] This was the Toutswe Culture and was centred on Toutswemogala, just north of the Lotsane River, making use of the good grazing lands on the eastern fringes of the Kalahari, especially during the higher rainfall cycle that occurred during this period. It is likely that it played an important role in supplying cattle to the Mapungubwe Kingdom, although the exotic trade beads, gold and cloth found at Mapungubwe have not been discovered in any Toutswe sites, suggesting that it was kept separate. The population seems to have declined near the end of the thirteenth century, probably due to the same Little Ice Age that affected Mapungubwe, and has been more sparsely settled ever since.

Most of the farms between Swartwater and Zanzibar on the South African side are narrow strips of land with a river frontage, about 500 hectares in size, that were called '*pondtplase*' (pound farms) because they were originally sold for one pound.

Roualeyn Gordon-Cumming must have been quite a figure – a dapper Scotsman with a bright red beard and often wearing a kilt in the field. As with many hunters of his time, before there was any thought of conservation, he shot game animals by the hundred, in an orgy of hunting that horrifies most of us today. Nevertheless, the record of his expedition along the Limpopo in 1846 gives us a great feeling of what the river was like in those days.

He was particularly interested in hippo, and we have selected two incidents in the Stockpoort area that tell us much about the man and the river, the latter being illustrated below.

14 June: 'At sundown the sea-cows [hippos] commenced their march up the river, passing opposite our camp, and making the most extraordinary sounds – blowing, snorting and roaring, sometimes crashing through the reeds, sometimes swimming gently, and splashing and sporting through the water. There being a little moonlight, I went down with my man Carey, and sat some time by the river-side, contemplating these wonderful monsters; it was a truly grand and very extraordinary scene; and the opposite bank of the stream being clad with trees of gigantic size and great beauty, they added greatly to the interest of the picture.'

18 June: 'Mist hung over the river, which as we advanced became more promising for sea-cow; at every turn there occurred deep, still pools and occasional sandy islands, densely clad with lofty reeds. Above and beyond these reeds stood trees of immense age and gigantic size, beneath which grew a long and very rank description of grass, on which the sea-cow delights to pasture.

'I soon found fresh spoor, and after holding on for several miles came, just as the sun was going

ABOVE: Gordon-Cumming attempts to anchor a hippo in the Limpopo River by cutting two parallel incisions into her thick hide in order to pull her towards the bank of the river where he later despatched her.

down, upon the fresh lairs of four hippopotami …

'I took the sea-cow next me, and with my first ball gave her a mortal wound, knocking loose the great plate on the top of her skull, when she commenced plunging round and round … I was now in a state of very great anxiety about my wounded sea-cow, for I feared that she would get into deep water, and be lost like the two last. To settle the matter, I fired a second shot from the bank … after which she kept constantly splashing round and round in a circle in the middle of the river. I had great fears of the crocodiles, and did not know whether the sea-cow might not attack me; my anxiety to secure her, however, overcame all hesitation so, divesting myself of my leathers [trousers], and armed with a sharp knife, I dashed into the water, which at first took me up to my arm-pits, but the middle was shallower.

'As I approached the behemoth I halted for a moment, ready to dive under the water if she attacked me; but though her eye looked very wicked, she was stunned, and did not know what she was doing; so, running in upon her, and seizing her short tail, I attempted to incline her course to land. It was extraordinary what enormous strength she still had in the water; I could not guide her in the slightest degree; and she continued to splash, plunge, and blow, and make her circular course, carrying me along with her, as if I was a fly on her tail … after some desperate hard work, sometimes pushing and sometimes pulling, the sea-cow continuing her circular course all the time, and I holding on like grim Death, eventually succeeded in bringing this gigantic and most powerful animal to the bank … I then sent a ball through the centre of her head, and she was numbered with the dead …'

Mmabolela Nature Reserve

Mmabolela is a private nature reserve established by newspaper magnate AV Lindbergh in 1913, through the consolidation of two large properties and two of the 'pondtplase'. The property today is owned by Mark and Sheila Berry. It includes the huge dark Mabalel pool, immortalised by Eugène Marais's haunting poem of the same name about a chief's daughter who is taken by a huge crocodile (see box on page 38). It is one of the best-known poems in the Afrikaans language. Willem van Riet wrote that the pool is over 7 miles (11 kilometres) long, consists of 'smooth, black water'; and is 'not short on sinister atmosphere'. He also saw three giant crocs that he estimated at least 17 feet (5.2 metres) long.

The pool, which is in fact some five kilometres long, is caused by a 'dyke' that acts as a natural weir, and just downstream are major rapids that give a roaring sound. These are the mysterious 'roaring waters' that Thomas Baines described in the nineteenth century, and called 'Impopo Mini'. The islands contain a number of Khami ruins and the site of where Baines camped. This particular stretch of the river comprises some of the finest examples of riverine habitat found anywhere along the Limpopo, untouched by the depredations of masses of elephants or human activity.

From Zanzibar and Platjan Border Post onwards the river enters one of the steepest drop-offs on the whole river, losing 100 metres in height in the 60 kilometres between here and where it opens out onto the flats just before the Motloutse confluence. The river is a sustained stretch of rapids, with many small streams and islets. Van Riet writes: 'Before now the rocks were just an irritation, but now the water accelerates and pours over numerous boulders and rocky ledges that obstruct the narrow stream between the high forested banks.' They regularly got caught up in branches and capsized. Eventually they returned to Zanzibar and organised a lift to the Motloutse.

Between the Zanzibar and Platjan Border Post is the crossing called Baines Drift. The drift was named in honour of Thomas Baines although he never crossed the Limpopo River at this point because it is clear from his diaries that he crossed it on his journey down from the Tati Goldfields more than 60 kilometres to the south-west. Nevertheless, the drift has been known as Baines Drift as far back as 1879 as recorded on F Jeppe's *Transvaal Map* of which Baines was a contributor. The drift was named in honour of him by Jeppe.

When visited by Hickman in 1967, the remains of a substantial fortification were still evident close to the drift, which he attributed to the defence of the drift against the Banyailand Trekkers in 1891 (although they actually tried to cross at Main Drift near Beit Bridge).

LEFT: Apart from the advent of the Pioneer Column of 1890, elephant hunting was the only major activity of European and Dutch ivory hunters.

FOLLOWING SPREAD: At the end of a long, dry winter one may encounter elephant seeking out the remaining water in the Limpopo riverbed between the Platjan Border Post and Sentinel Ranch.

Mmamagwa Hill

While conducting an elephant aerial survey in Botswana in 1976 Clive Walker noticed extensive walling on top of a large sugarloaf sandstone hill adjacent to the Motloutse River. He went to investigate, and later contacted the Botswana Museum in Gaborone, who were unaware of the site.

Enquiries among the local people showed that the resident Barbirwa regarded it with great respect and the two distinctive outcrops, known as Leeukop and Mapungubwe Hill (a separate one from Mapungubwe in South Africa), as sacred sites.

The hill is known as Mmamagwa and today is under the custodianship of Mashatu Game Reserve. It is indeed of great significance for it is very ancient, and was found to be one of the main centres of the Mapungubwe Kingdom based at Mapungubwe Hill 45 kilometres to the east in South Africa. However, no gold objects have been found to date, and this is probably one of the reasons why it has received less attention from archaeologists. There are still many interesting artefacts to be found on site, and Mmamagwa has a stunning wilderness setting that far eclipses its South African neighbour.

According to Grant Hall, who carried out archaeological research on the site,[3] it has been occupied by a number of cultural groups on and off for at least the last 50 000 years. The early inhabitants were Middle Stone Age people, who left scatters of tools on the surface. There are many pieces of pottery, some with distinct 'Zhizo', 'Leopards Kopje' and 'Mapungubwe' period markings on them, as well as burnishing and grinding stones, bits of animal bone from middens, the occasional ostrich eggshell and large blue European trade beads.

The various inhabitants have maintained dry stonewalling for 650 to 700 years, which was used to level terraces for huts and for small patches of crops, in addition to the obvious function of defence. The walling on top of the hill was used to separate the chief and his family, bodyguards and medicine men from the commoners, according to the Mapungubwe pattern of ritual seclusion. Much later in the eighteenth century, contact with white traders allowed various groups to obtain firearms, and some of the walls were modified to include loopholes for defence with firearms.

At the end of a ridge is a site with a particular 'sense of place'. There are several *marabaraba* boards carved out of the rock, and one can imagine the royal bodyguard sitting at this wonderful place, gazing out over the plains, and playing the board game to keep themselves occupied. Overhead is a medium-sized baobab, with a number of initials carved into its weathered trunk. It is thought that the initials CJR were carved by Cecil John Rhodes on one of his journeys past this area, with the initials of his aide Antonio de Silva just above.

There are also the grey soil patches from far more recent huts, Mmamagwa is interesting in that it was occupied right up to the 1940s, the local chief even claiming to have been born at the site.

Mogalakwena River

The name of the Mogalakwena River means 'the stronghold of the crocodile', and by this stage in our Limpopo journey crocodile are very much part of the picture. This river is particularly rich in history.

The upper part of the Mogalakwena is called the Nyl because when one of the early treks that set out to travel up Africa to the Holy Land, the Jerusalem Gangers (Jerusalem Travellers), reached the river in the vicinity of Nylstroom (now Modimolle), they seriously believed that they had arrived at the upper reaches of the Nile. Nylsvlei nearby is an internationally renowned wetland, and the number of waterbirds it attracts has led to it being listed as a RAMSAR site. Under the control of the Limpopo environmental authority, LEDET, it enjoys the support of one of the most dynamic non-governmental organisations in South Africa. The 'Friends of Nylsvei' represent the important role the private sector can and do play in support of a national asset.

Further on at Moorddrif the Nyl turns north and is called the Mogalakwena. Moorddrif is the site of the murder of two families that started the war with Chief Makapane, which ended in the tribe being starved out of the Makapans Caves. The caves are 15 kilometres to the east of the town of Mokopane (formerly Potgietersrus), and are also a World Heritage Site linked to Taung and the Cradle of Humankind, because they have produced a large number of fossils, including several hominids. This site represents more than three million years of fossil records including proto-humans and humans from *Australopithecine* to the present.

Over the mountains from Mokopane, on the Sterkrivier, which is also a tributary of the Mogalakwena, are the farms Doornhoek and Rietfontein, where the great poet and naturalist of the Waterberg, Eugène Marais, spent years observing baboons and termites, and made a pioneering contribution to the study of animal behaviour with his books *My Friends the Baboons* and *The Soul of the White Ant*.

Shortly after the Mogalakwena River the rapids cease, and the Limpopo flows more gently through sandy flats on to the Motloutse. Both sides of the river have newly created private game reserves, with the Tuli South Game Reserve on the Botswana side all the way up to the Motloutse. This is a particularly beautiful part of the river on the Botswana side with many farms going over to conservation and where one will encounter magnificent outcrops of granite hills and beautiful baobab trees, an area frequented by one of the authors over many years, and a section of the Vhembe Game Reserve on the South African side.

Motloutse River

Motloutse means 'the place of the large elephant' and it is now a relatively small river, with usually just a dry riverbed except for short periods during the rains. However, in the past it was probably far more important because it is thought to be one of the rivers (with the Shashe) that drained the Okavango and Upper Zambezi before the uplift of the Kalahari–Zimbabwe axis 60 million years ago.

A short distance upstream is the striking feature of Solomons Wall, a dyke of dark dolerite that falls off into the river. Further on is the important archaeological site of Mmamagwa (see box on page 93), which was one of the main sub-centres of the Mapungubwe Kingdom. Some 200 elephant have occupied this area as far south as Zanzibar Border Post and game species have steadily increased.

Approximately 70 kilometres upstream is the village of Bobonong, where the Pioneer Column established its main base camp and training centre before starting out to colonise 'Rhodesia' (see box on page 98).

There is a large baobab tree to the west of Fort Tuli that is covered with carved names and initials. This marks the remarkable passage of a private company to colonise a country. It was the original Rhodesian Pioneer Column of 1890, led by Frank Johnson and guided by famous hunter Frederick Courtney Selous.

The column had camped beneath the tree, watered their horses and marked their passing on the trunk of the baobab. One very clear name was that of WE Fry, the intelligence officer attached to the column, who wrote a book about his experiences. Today the tree is a national monument – a stone parapet protecting it from inquisitive elephants.

The Pioneer Column was paid for by Cecil Rhodes, whose British South Africa Company had managed against stiff competition to wheedle a concession out of Lobengula, the Matabele king in Bulawayo. On the strength of this concession Rhodes had obtained a Charter from the British Government to colonise the country, and Johnson had agreed to lead the column £87 500 and 80 000 hectares of choice farmland when they had reached Mashonaland. Rhodes sent his friend Dr Jameson along as adviser and representative of the Company.

Either Johnson or Selous (there is some debate who) suggested that they should skirt round to the east of the Matabele heartland, and thereby avoid conflict with Lobengula's warriors, who were not happy with the Concession at all, and seemed to be spoiling for a fight.

Selous had spent seven years hunting in Lobengula's country in the 1870s, and knew it well. By 1890 most of the big herds of elephants had gone, but Selous had criss-crossed the area on foot when it was still infested with tsetse fly and horses could therefore not be used. From initially being laughed at by Lobengula, because he had not even seen an elephant, Selous had become a hardened hunter, and some almost impossible narrow escapes had given him a reputation of invincibility. Combined with his intimate knowledge of the local blacks, and fluency in several languages, he was the ideal person to guide the brash and arrogant young Johnson through the countryside.

The Pioneer Column had established a major base and training camp on the Motloutse River, and set off along the route planned by Selous at the end of June 1890. They made an advanced base at Fort Tuli and, when Lobengula's envoys told them that they would be exterminated if they crossed the Shashe River, they mounted a demonstration with, of all things, a searchlight, together with a 9-pounder cannon and machine guns. This demonstration probably impressed the elders sufficiently that, athough Matabele warriors shadowed them for much of the time, they were not attacked in the ten weeks it took to reach their destination, Fort Salisbury, now Harare.

At that time Selous believed that the Tuli was the major river, and Shashe just a tributary. Therefore the stretch from the Tuli–Shashe confluence to the Limpopo confluence was called

'The Tuli', leading to the names 'Fort Tuli', 'Tuli Circle' and, later, the 'Tuli Block'.

The Pioneer Column did not actually travel along the Limpopo River (which interestingly enough Fry calls the Crocodile on his map of the Pioneer Column's route). From Fort Matlaputla (the present-day village of Bobonong), they went fairly straight to Fort Tuli, following a range of hills about 15–20 kilometres north of the Limpopo, gradually turning northwards after crossing the Shashe and the Umzimgwane.

The Pioneer Column was an interesting bunch of people. From the mass of applications Johnson had selected a cross-section of colonial society – clergymen, doctors, lawyers, prospectors and miners, sailors and tailors, builders and butchers – 'the complete nucleus of a self-contained civil population' as Johnson put it. The sandy drifts of the Shashe riverbed were quite an obstacle, and it took two days to move the force of less than 1 000 men across the river. The searchlight was set up every evening to play across the countryside, with land mines being detonated at intervals.

Apart from the constant fear of an Ndebele attack, the biggest headache for the column was the river crossings. During the fording of the Bubye, the wagon carrying the steam-engine for Fry's searchlight hit a stump and crashed upside down in the water. It was turned over again by the ingenious sailors from *HMS Boadicea* accompanying the column.

Abandoned since the turn of the century, Fort Tuli lies in the eastern-most corner of Botswana in the triangle bordered by the Shashe and Limpopo rivers. The only tribute to the pioneers at what remains of the silent fort on the road to Mashonaland is shattered glass and scattered iron. Many a secret lies forgotten in the peace and quiet of the surrounding mopane country. The Shashe, at this point, is a sandy stretch some 500 metres wide with clean, clear water running close to the fort side of the bank.

FAR LEFT: Cecil John Rhodes – love him, hate him or ignore him – there is no denying this man left an indelible mark on the southern African landscape.

LEFT: Officers of the Pioneer Column led by Major Frank Johnston (seated centre) and Frederick Selous, scout, writer and intelligence officer (seated extreme right).

There remains just one free-ranging, flourishing elephant population on private land south of the Zambezi River – the elephants of Botswana's Tuli Block. Many people feel that there are too many elephants there, but it wasn't always so.

The first white man known to have hunted elephants on the Limpopo was the renegade Coenraad de Buys in 1809. Records are scanty but he appears to have been a fearless hunter, dispatching elephant at close quarters with an ancient muzzleloader. He was followed by trade explorers, such as David Hume, who penetrated as far as the Shashe River. In their northward movement, the Transvaal Boers were not slow to dispose of elephants either. Petrus Jacobs brought down 200 elephants in one expedition alone.

Between 1846 and 1848 Roualeyn Gordon-Cumming (see box on page 90) conducted two hunting expeditions into the Tuli area, and shot a number of elephants between the Shoshong and the Motloutse rivers, and along the Limpopo.

Following in the wake of hunters were the traders, who swapped guns for ivory with African chiefs and headmen. What the tribesmen lacked in shooting skill they made up for in patience, bush craft and a thorough understanding of game. By 1855 elephants were so scarce in the Tuli area that hunters such as Baldwin, Oswell, Finaughty and Selous had to venture much further north. By the time Selous led the Pioneer Column into Mashonaland in July 1890, the country was empty of elephant. From the Motloutse to the Shashe no elephants were to be observed for the next 50 years.

Part of the territory from which the elephants had been hunted out was negotiated, one report states, 'wheedled' out of Khama the Great by Chamberlain in 1895 for a railway strip 10 to 12 miles (16 to 19 kilometres) wide along the Limpopo River. Khama was assured, 'We will take the land we want for the railway, and no more, and if we take any of his garden ground (we will not take much), we will give him compensation elsewhere.'

In fact Chamberlain was not telling the truth for there was at the time no intention of building a railway line but rather it was to be given to the British South Africa Company (BSAC) as part of the continuous Rhodesian frontier strip with one objective being to launch the Jameson Raid on Johannesburg. After the failure of the Jameson Raid, the BSAC lost the right to govern the 'railway strip' as part of Rhodesia. It was only in 1903 that the BSAC began surveying the strip for white farms. Ownership was confirmed in the name of the company by government proclamation of 1904–1905. In 1912 the company started advertising the farms for sale but World War I held the effort up and by 1920 the Ngwato lost all sovereignty to the land which became known as the 'Tuli Block'.

Khama's concession included the 40 000 hectares lying to the west of the Shashe River, today known as the Tuli Circle of Zimbabwe which is in use as a controlled hunting area administered by the Zimbabwe Department of National Parks and Wildlife Conservation. It was originally granted as a 10-mile (16-kilometre) exclusion zone to protect the cattle of the Fort from the spread of 'lung-sickness' which had broken out among the Bamangwato cattle in 1891. It has remained a somewhat illogical part of Rhodesia/Zimbabwe ever since.

Although elephants were not seen in the Tuli area for so many decades, they had not disappeared forever. In the 1940s a Dr Nel of Pietersburg became the first Tuli landowner to sight the return of the huge animals.

Elephants began to move in steadily from the north and west from that time. By 1956 Bechuanaland (now Botswana) had an established game department which, like many other similar departments, was formed in order to control elephants in tribal and farming areas – an operation that eventually accounted for the deaths of 1 800 elephants. Bechuanaland's policy was to control the elephants east of the railway line, containing them in areas to which the local communities would consent.

What started the big movement of elephants into this corner of Botswana? Rhodesia had begun to control elephants on tribal lands, while the Transvaal farmers owning land along the Limpopo were reportedly shooting indiscriminately. Hounded by the gun and diminishing habitat, the elephants began retreating into the Tuli enclave – there was nowhere else for them to go.

The Tuli became their final home and they have since re-colonised their old haunts across the Limpopo River in present-day Mapungubwe National Park. They also colonised communal land and Sentinal Ranch on the Zimbabwean side of the Limpopo River. They have also moved south across the Motloutse River as far as Baines Drift. There are now some 1 200 elephants in the Tuli of which about 600 are permanent residents – and the number is growing. A survey of the elephants and their impact on the habitat originally commenced in 1976, conducted by Bruce Page who at the time was a Master's student at Wits University.

A subsequent study on the population dynamics of elephants was undertaken by Jeanetta Seliers over many years. Mopane, as may well be assumed, is heavily utilised in certain areas, large lala palm trees have largely disappeared as have various other species, and many *Commiphoras* have been uprooted (as is now taking place in the Mapungubwe National Park).

Pressure of elephant numbers has been relieved by the opening up of the Mapungubwe National Park across the river, as well as Tuli South Game Reserve. Elephants will clearly be a major feature of the new Transfrontier Park linking conservation areas in the three countries.

Northern Tuli Game Reserve

From the Motloutse on to the Shashe, conservation areas predominate, with the well-established Northern Tuli Game Reserve (or Tuli Block) on the Botswana side, and the private reserves of Ratho and Vhembe on the South African side, with some irrigation lands next to the river, and then the new Mapungubwe National Park after Pont Drift. The river banks on the Botswana side are particularly steep from the Motloutse to the junction of the Shashe and Limpopo.

During the last half century, the Northern Tuli Game Reserve has played a hugely important role in the conservation of large game, especially elephants (see box on page 100), and has conserved a reservoir of animals while South Africa was playing political games about whether this part of the Limpopo Valley should have

The Zeederberg Coach Route[6]

During the Colonial Period, the Eastern Tuli area was an important thoroughfare between the Cape or the Transvaal and Zimbabwe (formerly Rhodesia). The drift across the Limpopo was known as Rhodes Drift, and was often used by Rhodes and his supporters.

After the occupation of Mashonaland in July 1890, Cecil John Rhodes commissioned Doel Zeederberg to establish a coach route from Pietersburg (now Polokwane) to Fort Salisbury and Bulawayo via Fort Tuli – the staging post for the Pioneer Column's entry into Mashonaland and Matabeleland. Towards the end of 1890 he built a drift across the Limpopo River, which was

named Rhodes Drift, and today is to be found within the Mapungubwe National Park. On the banks of the Limpopo River on the Botswana side, Rhodes is reputed to have carved his initials into a Mashatu tree which, if it ever existed, is certainly no longer there.

When the river came down in flood, crossing the Limpopo was quite a hazardous undertaking. On several occasions the water went over the floorboards, and the passengers had to perch on top of the coach (what a pity this scene was not captured in a photograph – it must have looked really dramatic).

Due to the heavy rains that year, resulting in sustained flooding, Zeederberg was forced to construct a pont at a spot upstream of Rhodes Drift, which he opened in February of 1891. It was named Pont Drift, which it is still called to this day. The pont lasted until 1960, when it disappeared in a Limpopo flood, and was replaced by a cable car for use when the river is high. During the dry season the sandy riverbed can be easily crossed by 4x4 vehicles.

a large conservation area or not. It was formed into an integrated game reserve in 1964 comprising 35 farms conserving an area of some 71 000 hectares today, with centralised management.

Tourism in Tuli started around 1970, with Tuli Lodge and Mashatu on different properties. They have both changed ownership since, but these two operations have grown to become flagship lodges and tented camps of the reserve. It has now become a core area of the Greater Mapungubwe Transfrontier Conservation area.

In addition to its importance in conservation, the Tuli area has played a key role in history, particularly at the end of the nineteenth century, with the Pioneer Column passing through it (see box on page 98), the route to the north followed by the Zeederberg Coach (see box below), and the early engagements of the Anglo-Boer War (see box on page 106).

After Pont Drift the coach proceeded to Bryce's Store, some 12 kilometres north of the Limpopo River, alongside the Pitsane River which had a spring that provided year-round water. The enterprising Bryce had established the store to serve the incoming traffic, and did a good trade for several years. After the store the coach went on to Fort Tuli, Rhodesia's first town.

The heavy rains of 1891/92 resulted in massive hold-ups at Fort Tuli of people, wagons and goods, for the wide Shashe River is in itself a difficult river to cross when in spate. Fortunately, it is not a deep-flowing river like the Limpopo, and it drops fairly quickly.

The journey from Pretoria to Bulawayo took five and a half days on the Transvaal Mail Coach. One can only imagine the aches and pains of these intrepid passengers when the coach finally pulled into its destination. It left Pretoria on a Sunday morning at 05:00 and arrived in Bulawayo at 10:00 on Friday. There was also a bi-weekly coach departing on a Wednesday. The fare was £22.10 (±R40).

Zeederberg passenger coaches were of an American design, pulled by teams of 10 or 12 horses or mules. The landed cost of each coach from America was £5 500 (±R10 000), a very considerable sum in those days. The driver and his assistant sat on top, as did any overflow of passengers. A good example of a Zeederberg coach type may be seen today in Museum Africa in Johannesburg.

Operating coaches in this terrain was somewhat hazardous and collisions with wild animals were common. Sometimes horses or mules were killed, and coaches wrecked by elephants. Coaches were also attacked by highwaymen when negotiating heavy patches of sand or rock, and a number of passengers had all their valuables stolen.

The Zeederberg coach service to Bulawayo was relatively short lived, however. Six years after it started, the service was immobilised by the rinderpest. The coach route was littered with abandoned wagons and the carcasses of hundreds of oxen killed by the disease. Then in 1897 the main railway line from Kimberley reached Bulawayo, and wealthier passengers preferred to go by the far more comfortable train.

During the Anglo-Boer War, the middle Limpopo/Eastern Tuli area played an important role, especially in the early days of the war. Although the battles were relatively small in scale, the presence of British troops in the area caused the Boers to station large numbers of urgently needed men (some say as many as 15 000) in the northern and north-western parts of the South African Republic, which lessened the pressure on the hard-pressed British forces in Mafikeng, Kimberley, Natal and elsewhere.

Commandant General Grobler had orders to immobilise the railway line to Bulawayo, but two main factors seem to have caused the failure of this mission. First, he only discussed it with the Zoutpansberg Commando and not with the Waterberg Commando who were very independent and seem to have effectively refused to move outside of the Transvaal. Second, in General van Rensburg he seems to have had a particularly weak, indecisive and almost cowardly leader of the Zoutpansberg Commando.

Both sides feared that the other would invade through the Tuli area. The British feared that the Boers would advance to blow up the railway line to Bulawayo, interfere with their Rhodesian mining interests, and possibly cause an uprising of the local populations of Rhodesia and Bechuanaland. The Boers feared a British invasion into their territory from the north. In fact, the British were rather effective in preying on these fears. Colonel Baden-Powell, the British commander, wrote a letter to a friend on the Limpopo referring mysteriously to an imaginary 'third column', knowing that the letter would be intercepted and read by the Boers!

The British forces in the area were mostly the 1 500 men of Colonel Baden-Powell's Rhodesian Regiment that was recruited in Bulawayo. Their main base was at Fort Tuli on the Shashe River, from where they set up outposts at and near Pont Drift and the nearby Rhodes Drift.

There were a number of engagements between groups of several hundred British and Boer troops, including the successful bombardment and capture of Bryce's Store 10 kilometres to the north of Pont Drift. Some prisoners and supplies were captured and men were killed and wounded, including Captain Leslie Blackburn, an imperial officer in charge of a British patrol, whose grave is in the Pioneer Cemetery at Fort Tuli. It is said that his position (hiding under a bush) was given away by an African tracker with the Boers who pointed out his boots! Generally the British were on the 'receiving' end, but it must be remembered that they kept a considerably superior force inactive during a critical time in the war.

There are a number of fortified hilltops to be seen throughout the Eastern Tuli area, as far as the Motloutse River, including the gun emplacements on Pitsani Hill from where Bryce's Store was shelled. Rifle and field-gun cartridges, buttons, bottles and squashed food tins have been picked up in several sites.

The Boers failed to follow up on their early victories, and did not advance on Fort Tuli, apparently due to weak leadership, and eventually withdrew from the area. Later a reconnaissance patrol across the river under the British commander at Fort Tuli, Col. Plumer, on 1 December 1899 was reported to be the first British force to enter enemy territory during the war.

PREVIOUS SPREAD: A large flock of Egyptian geese, *Alopochen aegyptiacus*, take flight across the Limpopo River. These very noisy birds are a welcome sight along the river and its tributaries.

LEFT TOP: The only access in or out of Botswana during periods when the Limpopo is in flood is via this cable car at the border post of Pont Drift. There have been occasions when the river has been so high, river craft have had to be used.

LEFT MIDDLE: Frederick Courtney Selous, 19th-century famous hunter, explorer and writer, was the intelligence officer of the Pioneer Column of 1890 (see box on page 98).

LEFT BOTTOM: The original site, 'Rhodes Drift' on the Botswana bank where Cecil Rhodes and party would stop over and rest under a giant mashatu tree where it is reputed he carved his initials. This was the site of the original crossing into the Tuli Block en route to what became Fort Tuli.

ABOVE TOP: The names of some members of the Pioneer Column of 1890 carved into a baobab tree on the way to Tuli Block. This tree is on the banks of the Shashe River, mistakenly believed to be the Tuli River.

ABOVE BOTTOM: The grave site of Captain Leslie Blackburn, who lies buried in the Pioneer Cemetery at Fort Tuli. He was one of the first casualties at the outbreak of the Anglo-Boer War of 1898.

FOLLOWING PAGE LEFT: Magnificent sightings of leopard may be had in the Mashatu Game Reserve in the north-eastern Tuli Block.

Shashe River

The Shashe River is important in its own right, because it is the largest tributary in the upper part of the Limpopo River. It's even more important role in the past, when draining the Okavango and Upper Zambezi, has been outlined in the Appendix on page 234.

The establishment of Fort Tuli is described in the box on page 98. The Shashe also played an important role in the Story of Gold, because many of the surface workings that yielded gold for Mapungubwe and Great Zimbabwe were up on the Zimbabwean Plateau. Henry Hartley showed many of these old diggings to his friend Carl Mauch and Thomas Baines, who then published somewhat premature claims about how many people would make their fortunes in the new goldfields to the north.[8]

In 1868 the New Victoria Goldfields on the Tati River in Botswana (which flows into the Shashe near present-day Francistown) were the first commercial goldfields in southern Africa, but these proved to be disappointing. In fact, all the mines in Zimbabwe and eastern Botswana were marginal at best, and no Europeans got rich from mining them, even though people continued mining on a small scale for a hundred years afterwards.

Early Hunters

Hunters have operated in the Limpopo Valley for more than a thousand years, but it was only in the nineteenth century that they wrote down their experiences. The first expeditions to be written up fairly quickly in books were those of Andrew Smith's expedition of 1835 and Cornwallis Harris's of 1836, both of whom just passed the Crocodile–Marico confluence, but did not really visit this section of the river. The Cornwallis-Harris expedition was certainly not the first hunting expedition to the Limpopo Valley, as suggested by Bartle Bull,[9] but it was the first safari that was written up in detail, at least in English,[10] and it captured the imagination of a whole generation of aspirant adventurers in England and its colonies.

Meanwhile, local hunters such as Henry Hartley started hunting along the Limpopo in the early 1840s, unfortunately not recording much of their experiences. In 1846 the flamboyant Scotsman R Gordon-Cumming made an extended expedition to the area,[11] firing off thousands of rounds of ammunition in what can only be described as a wanton slaughter, taking many shots to kill elephants, and wounding many animals. An example is the following quote: '… two first-rate bull elephants and one hippopotamus fell to my rifle this day. I fought one of the former in dense wait-a-bit jungle from half-past eleven till the sun was under, when his tough old spirit fled, and he fell pierced with fifty-seven balls …'

Cummings's colourful account, such as his amazing battle with his first hippopotamus (see box on page 90) caught the imagination even more, but he also provided very useful observations of this section of the Limpopo. He often reports buffalo, sometimes in huge herds numbering several hundred, which are now extinct in this part of the world. He regularly saw both white and black rhino, tsessebe, and even a gemsbok (which is seldom seen this far east), and was very taken by the magnificent sable antelope.

Cummings also made some contribution to science. For example, he admired, and was one of the first people to record, the 'bushbuck of the Limpopo', which he

Timeline of events in the Olifants Drift to the Tuli Section

1836	1846-8	1871	1872–80
Cornwallis Harris travels to the Magaliesberg and up along the Crocodile to near its confluence with the Marico.	R Gordon-Cumming and Oswell-Vardon travel on separate hunts all up and down this section of the river.	Baines travels briefly along the river en route from the Tati goldfields to Pretoria and carves his name on a large baobab tree, the site of one of his camps.	Selous leaves Kimberley on his first hunting trip into southern Africa.

11 October 1899	23 October 1899	2 November 1899	May 1902
Anglo-Boer War declared.	First engagement in the Anglo-Boer War in Tuli area; Captain Leslie Blackburn killed.	Bryce's Store Battle in the Anglo-Boer War.	Treaty of Vereeniging signed to end Anglo-Boer War.

called by the outlandish name of *Serolomootlooques*. Although he claimed it as a new species, it is now recognised as a separate subspecies, which still bears his name *Tragelaphus scriptus roualeynei* (the Limpopo bushbuck).

Cummings made a huge profit on his hunting expeditions, largely because the game, and especially elephants, were so plentiful and not yet used to hunters' guns. However, they exacted a huge toll in animals and people. In four expeditions he recorded that he lost 45 horses and 70 cattle, mostly to horse-sickness, 70 hunting dogs to a variety of causes, and one of his trusted servants to a lion, plucked from where he was sleeping next to the fire.

Many of the hunters who were to become household names, such as Jan Viljoen, William Baldwin, William Finaughty and Selous, only arrived in the area after 1850, when the game populations were being rapidly wiped out. By 1855 elephants had been virtually hunted out of this section of the river, and in the early 1870s Selous had to move deeper into Mashonaland to find elephants. By 1890 there was very little game of any type on this stretch of the river.

FOLLOWING SPREAD: The long dark pool of Mmabolela surrounded by lush riverine vegetation immortalised by Eugene Marais in his famous poem of the same name. See page 91.

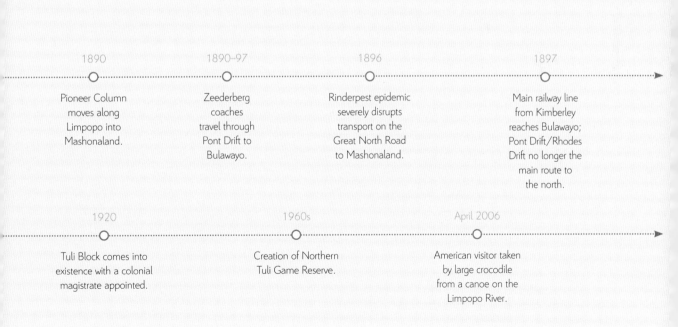

1890	1890–97	1896	1897
Pioneer Column moves along Limpopo into Mashonaland.	Zeederberg coaches travel through Pont Drift to Bulawayo.	Rinderpest epidemic severely disrupts transport on the Great North Road to Mashonaland.	Main railway line from Kimberley reaches Bulawayo; Pont Drift/Rhodes Drift no longer the main route to the north.

1920	1960s	April 2006
Tuli Block comes into existence with a colonial magistrate appointed.	Creation of Northern Tuli Game Reserve.	American visitor taken by large crocodile from a canoe on the Limpopo River.

CHAPTER 4

Limpopo–Shashe Confluence & Mapungubwe

> 'The Limpopo is ... one of those mysteriously
> important, eastern flowing rivers of Africa ...
> It has played its part in the rise of humanity
> and the history of Black Africa.'
>
> – MONTGOMERY, DSH, 1992, TWO SHORES OF THE OCEAN

We stood quietly on a newly constructed platform absorbing the tranquillity of a red Limpopo sunset and gazing out over the wonderful scenery of the Limpopo–Shashe confluence. On our left the setting sun sank ever lower over the dry bed of the Limpopo River, with its tall gallery forest of fig, mashatu and thorn trees, as it wound out of sight in the flat landscape. In front of us were two islands, the larger, well-vegetated Sinwahare Island in Botswana, and more to the right the rocky Beacon Island with its white survey beacon proclaiming the point where South Africa, Botswana and Zimbabwe come together.

Behind the Sinwahare Island was the huge expanse of the Shashe River, many times wider than the Limpopo, its width of sand giving a clue to its ancient status as the largest river in the whole of southern Africa. Further downstream the landscape was quite different, dominated by sandstone koppies glowing red in the setting sun, with the combined river flowing off to the east. Over our shoulders to the right the familiar outline of Mapungubwe Hill, and to the left the glow of the lights from the Venetia Diamond Mine.

After the sun had finally disappeared in the west we were doing a final scan with our binoculars before packing up when we noticed a group of elephants in the distance setting off purposefully across the Shashe River from the Botswana/Tuli side. As we watched a few more set out, and more, until there was a whole line of elephants strung out across the expanse of sand to where they disappeared into the trees on the Zimbabwe side. By the time it was too dark to make them out in the gathering dusk, we had counted no less than 146 elephants crossing over.

PREVIOUS SPREAD: Young Colin Norton, sitting on one of the prominent outcrops in the park, has an excellent view of both the Shashe and Limpopo rivers in the distance.

The Journey Continues

The confluence of two major rivers is always a site of interest, and often a site with a strong aura, resonance or sense of place. This is recognised by many indigenous peoples, and confluences are often said to be sites where the ancestral spirits live, where one can communicate with forefathers. Some people talk about 'energy fields', 'ley lines' and other sources of inspiration that we do not entirely understand, but can often feel when we are there.

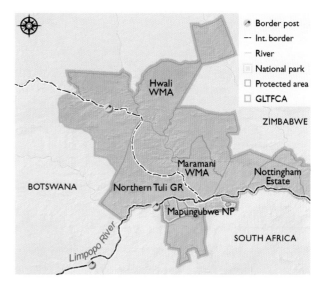

With its wide sweep of the sandy Shashe approaching from the north-west, the fig trees and baobabs, the islands at the confluence itself, and the orange-coloured sandstone koppies ideally placed for appreciating views and sunsets, the Limpopo–Shashe confluence viewpoint is probably the best site of all to view the Limpopo River. Thousands of people have already sat at this site and appreciated the atmosphere and, as a recently created national park, with a picnic site and confluence viewing platforms, it is likely to become one of the most visited sites in the middle Limpopo Valley.

LEFT: This sketch illustrates the far greater width of the Shashe River compared with the Limpopo as the two rivers converge opposite the Mapungubwe National Park.

Why is Mapungubwe so important?

The World Heritage Site Nomination Document records the following key features:

- Mapungubwe was the centre of the **first powerful indigenous kingdom in southern Africa, starting more than 1 000 years ago**.
- There are over **400 archaeological sites**. The main centres during the Mapungubwe period were Schroda, K2 and Mapungubwe itself, with secondary centres at Leokwe and Mmamagwa.
- The kingdom grew as a result of wealth created from **trade with the Indian Ocean network, combined with a Nile-type flooding system** that supported enough agriculture to feed a population of over 9 000 people.
- **Trade goods** found at Mapungubwe come from as far afield as **China, Persia and India**, and included gold, glass beads, cotton cloth, Chinese ceramics, ivory, copper and hides. Many are housed in the **Mapungubwe Museum**, University of Pretoria.
- By the thirteenth century AD, **a new type of social hierarchy** had developed and impacted on the landscape. Mapungubwe Hill was occupied and modified to separate the leader and his elite from the commoners below.
- The onset of the Little Ice Age caused drought and crop failures. The kingdom dispersed after AD 1300, new social and political alliances were formed, and the centre of regional power shifted to Great Zimbabwe. **Mapungubwe was therefore the forerunner of the Great Zimbabwe Culture.**[1]

The Mapungubwe Story[2]

At school most of us were given the impression that 'civilisation' has existed in Europe and the Middle East for thousands of years, but 'history' in the southern part of Africa only really started when Van Riebeeck landed at the Cape in 1652. How exciting then to find out that our African heritage is much richer than that – more than 700 years ago there was a sophisticated town of over 5 000 people living close to the Limpopo–Shashe confluence, who had taken over control of the trade routes to the coast, and used the wealth accumulated to set up an organised society, with clear differentiation between the commoners and their 'sacred' leader living on top of the hill now known as Mapungubwe, the 'place of many jackals'.

The first capital was at Schroda (named after the farm where the archaeological site was found), which was settled by the Zhizo people (characterised by the pottery pattern first found at Zhizo in Zimbabwe) in about AD 900, towards the end of the prolonged dry period that lasted from about AD 600–1000. Cattle dung and bones dug up at the site, together with grindstones and remains of grain bins, showed that the occupants were cattle and small stock farmers who also planted crops. However, the fact that they arrived *before* the end of the dry period, and the presence of substantial debris from working ivory, suggests that they were first attracted by the elephant herds, which are still a key feature of the broader area today. Already in those days elephants may have been a problem to crop farmers, since most of the Zhizo settlements were well away from the river, which would have been the main elephant habitat with lala palms and tall shade-and-fruit trees. It seems that the night-time raids by elephants experienced recently by the Maramani community in Zimbabwe may have been part of community life for hundreds of years.

BELOW: A series of viewing platforms have been erected on a high sandstone ridge, affording superb views of the river and surrounding countryside of Zimbabwe, Botswana and back into the Park.

Estimates suggest that in its heyday about 300–500 people lived at Schroda, which was the largest settlement in the area at the time. A wonderful collection of clay figurines of wild animals, cattle, fantasy creatures and fertility symbols (now mostly housed in the National Cultural History Museum in Pretoria) suggest that Schroda was also the centre for female initiation ceremonies.

Schroda was the first settlement where substantial numbers of trade beads were found, showing that its inhabitants had already linked into the Indian Ocean trading network.

In about AD 1000 the area was taken over by people from the south whose culture has been called Leopard's Kopje because of their pottery style. They established a new, larger capital at the site known as K2, which is the unimaginative name given to it by one of the early archaeologists.

K2 housed up to 1 500 people, and was organised in the well-known Central Cattle Pattern, with residential huts set out in a conventional layout round the central cattle kraal. This showed the pivotal role of cattle in society, and the cattle kraal was also the main gathering place and court of the chief, who lived among the commoners.

Excavations at K2 show that the people were working copper and ivory, had iron knives and tools, were manufacturing cotton cloth (as shown by the clay spindle whorls) and were trading beads. At this stage they were melting a large number of imported small beads together in small clay moulds to make the unique much larger 'garden-roller beads', which have only ever been found at sites associated with the Mapungubwe civilisation.

K2 is situated in an enclosed valley of limited size. After 200 years the numbers of people had grown and society had changed substantially, with cattle becoming less central to community life, and the tremendous wealth generated from the Indian Ocean trade had turned the chief and his immediate family into an elite that had less and less to do with the commoners. In order to separate the chief more effectively, the capital moved one kilometre to the north-east, to Mapungubwe.

The very different nature of the Mapungubwe site allowed the chief to assume the role of sacred leader, and keep himself apart by living on top of the hill, which was an established rainmaking site. By doing this he would have acquired the power of the site, and reinforced his link with rainmaking.

The change in the shape of the landscape in which the town was situated seems to reflect how the people thought about their leader. In K2 the town was in a valley, with the king near the middle, mixing with the people, being 'one of us'. From this they moved a short way to a landscape where he was still at the centre, but lifted above the people, on the 'pedestal' of Mapungubwe Hill; he was mystical, remote and directly in touch with the ancestors and the bringing of rain.

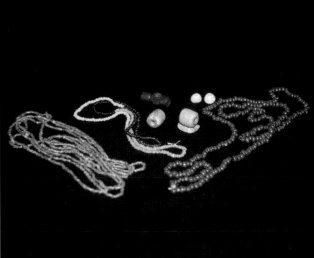

At Mapungubwe there were about 5 000 people scattered around the hill itself, on the southern terrace and on the plateau to the east. A further 4 000 lived nearby, with a substantial number living close to the crops on the floodplains on both sides of the Limpopo River.

The chief gained great riches from both the direct trade in ivory, gold from Zimbabwe, rhino horn, leopard skins and iron, as well as the tax that traders had to pay when moving along the trade routes through Mapungubwe. This is shown by the huge numbers of beads and gold objects found at the grave sites, particularly the three royal graves on top of the hill.

The conditions that allowed this major capital to develop all came together at the Limpopo–Shashe confluence, and at the right time in relation to other events in southern Africa. These were conditions for sufficient agricultural crop production, good stock farming, suitable rocky habitat to separate an elite ruler, for rainmaking, and for the southward extension of the Indian Ocean trade.

ABOVE LEFT: The hidden treasures of Mapungubwe revealed a high skill of gold craftsmanship, especially in the beautifully crafted paper-thin gold foil of a rhinoceros mounted on wood (The Golden Rhino).

ABOVE RIGHT: Trade beads from the K2 site of Mapungubwe dating from AD 800. The beads originated in the East transported across the Indian Ocean by wooden dhows, and then using African intermediaries travelling overland – then finally up the Limpopo River to Mapungubwe.

ABOVE: Extensive irrigation may be found along the Limpopo Province side of the river, extending back upstream to as far as the Groblersbrug/Martins Drift border crossing between South Africa and Botswana.

The first national reserve along this part of the Limpopo was the Dongola Botanical Reserve, which later became the Dongola Wildlife Sanctuary. The story is an interesting one in the annals of wildlife conservation in South Africa, not because of what it achieved (which was minimal), but in what went *wrong*, how it illustrates the politics of the time, and how it relates to the characters involved.

The initial concept came from government botanist Dr Illtyd Buller Pole Evans. He was a Welshman who made a major contribution to botany in South Africa. Pole Evans saw the benefits of reserves to protect and study representative examples of veld, pasture grasses and ecological processes. He recommended a Botanical Survey of the Union, which included a range of botanical reserves throughout the country. In this he received enthusiastic support from Jan Smuts, who was a neighbour of his at Irene in Pretoria. The two had become firm friends through their passion for botany.

One of the sites identified by Pole Evans was close to the Limpopo River west of Messina, and initially included a block of nine farms, with the prominent Dongola Kop in the north-east corner. Because of this it became known as the Dongola Botanical Reserve when it was established in 1922 to 'conserve the wildlife and natural vegetation'.

Within a few years the reserve was looking quite different from the surrounding farms which were severely overgrazed, and the game populations were increasing. Pole Evans invited a number of prominent people to visit the reserve, and gained their support for adding more farms to the original nine. By 1944 it had grown to 44 farms covering 60 000 hectares. Experiments conducted there under Pole Evans's direction had also led to the development of Limpopo grass, *Echinochloa pyramidalis*, as a hay grass and for stabilising loose sand.

Pole Evans took a personal interest in the Dongola Botanical Reserve, and visited it often, but when he was away Mr AB Emery, the manager of the Messina Copper Mine, acted as honorary caretaker. Emery had privately bought four farms along the Limpopo River, which he used as a hunting and recreation area, while keeping a few cattle.

Some years later Pole Evans and Emery fell out. During a drought Emery had moved his cattle onto one of the most picturesque farms of the reserve, Belvedere, without permission. He was pumping water from the precious spring, and destroying the surrounding vegetation by overgrazing.

In the 1920s and '30s Pole Evans was encouraged by the number of national parks being created by the Nationalist Party government, and he began to work on creating a national park with the Dongola Botanical Reserve as the core. When Jan Smuts came back into power, the two of them started to push more strongly for a park, with the assistance of the controversial Andrew Conroy, Smuts's Minister of Lands and Irrigation. They were rather surprised when the National Parks Board showed very little interest in the project, and in fact some were actively opposed to it, on the grounds that they were already struggling to manage Kruger National Park, which contained similar habitats. The board was dominated by Nationalist Party members, and this gave a clear indication of the political storm that was brewing.

In the meanwhile, Pole Evans, Conroy and Smuts pressed ahead with their plans. The new proposal was for a huge area of 123 farms, totalling more than 240 000 hectares and including more than 100 kilometres of the southern bank of the Limpopo River from near Beit Bridge to Ratho, well to the west of Pont Drift. It is also interesting that prominent figures from Southern Rhodesia (now Zimbabwe) and the Bechuanaland Protectorate (now Botswana) were taken to the area or approached, to create corresponding reserves on the northern side of the Limpopo River. Thus the concept for the Limpopo–Shashe Transfrontier Conservation Area, which has recently been established, has been around for more than 60 years. Unfortunately this was anathema to the Nationalists, who didn't want anything to do with British colonies, and further exacerbated the tensions.

In October 1944 Conroy published his intentions to set aside the area to be called the Dongola Wildlife Sanctuary (DWS). This created an uproar, and led to some of the most acrimonious debates in Parliament up to that time. The major argument was that 'valuable' agricultural land was being alienated for wildlife conservation, but there were a number of secondary issues such as the spread of stock diseases, which is still a key issue in the establishment of Transfrontier Conservation Areas (TFCAs) today. In addition, there were accusations that Pole Evans and the politicians were merely trying to establish a cushy hunting farm for themselves at government expense! This does seem to resonate with reports of Nationalist cabinet ministers hunting elephants in the area in the 1970s and '80s!

Emery came into the picture again. While he had been one of the farmers campaigning in the 1920s and '30s for the price of their farms (and therefore their Land Bank loans) to be reduced to an eighth of their original price, he now used his influence to persuade people how valuable this same land was when faced with a threat of expropriation!

The Select Committee appointed to investigate the issue could not resolve it, but recommended that the size of the sanctuary should be reduced to less than half that of the original proposal. A Parliamentary vote went more or less along party lines, and the Dongola Wildlife Sanctuary Act was published in March 1947. Trustees were appointed, money was raised, farms were acquired and negotiations with neighbouring countries began.

However, it was all short lived. Not only had Smuts misread the support for the DWS, he had also misread support for his own party. In fact the DWS was one of the key election issues that brought the Nationalists to power in 1948, and one of the first things they did was to repeal the Dongola Wildlife Sanctuary Act. Soon afterwards the farms were returned to their original owners, money was given back to donors, and the farms making up the DWS were allocated to settlers. As Jane Carruthers put it: 'Settlers returned to carp about the poor farming conditions of the area, Emery to entertain his friends with shooting parties and dances at Skutwater – indeed it was soon as though nothing had ever disturbed the tranquillity of the far north-western Transvaal.'

How to Feed all these People

One of the key issues in the change from scattered villages to a large concentration of people in an organised town was the production of enough food. If one looks out over the veld now, it is very difficult to imagine how sufficient crops could be grown using the simple farming techniques available at the time. The irrigation pivots down next to the Limpopo River tell us that the soils are good, but present-day farming is only made possible by extensive irrigation systems and use of fertilisers. In the days of Mapungubwe there appear to be two main reasons why the area could support sufficient crops to support so many people.

First, studies of the rainfall show that it has fluctuated substantially over the last millennium, with the total annual rainfall mostly well above the present average of around 350 mm. In particular, there is evidence that there was a sustained wet period from around AD 1000–1300, which is exactly the period during which the Mapungubwe Kingdom developed to its full extent. The significance of this is that sorghum and millet, the staple crops that were available at the time (maize only arrived in this part of Africa after AD 1500), generally require about 500 mm of annual rainfall to flourish. So for most of this period the rainfall would have been above this critical threshold for the key staple crops.

Second, it is likely that there was regular flooding of the floodplain, caused by floodwaters backing up from the waters of the Shashe itself, as well as from the rocky narrows at the confluence and at Poachers' Corner. This flooding and slowing down of the water flow would have caused the silt load in the river to be deposited on the lands of the floodplain, and would therefore have enriched the soil on a regular basis, possibly even annually. If this is the case it could have been close to a Nile-type of flooding and soil replenishment system. During wetter years even now the water is said to flow 'backwards' (from east to west) in the Kolope floodplains on the farm Samaria.

Both of these factors would therefore have allowed substantial crops of sorghum and millet to be grown in the first place, and then to be grown over and over again on the same lands without exhausting the soil, due to the regular flooding and soil replenishment.

OPPOSITE: The Mapungubwe National Park has provided a wonderful canopy walk to a bird hide alongside the Limpopo River, providing a joyful opportunity to spot birds and identify tree species, as well as the chance to see the river up close.

Stock Farming

The early hunter-gatherers probably ate a much more balanced diet than the tribes that followed them, including a wide range of bulbs, roots, fruit, nuts and even insects (grubs, larvae and mopane worms), supplemented by meat from hunting. This is what the San 'first peoples' inhabiting the Mapungubwe area would have lived on. However, densities of people were limited by the overall low quantities of food available in the landscape.

When the Iron Age Bantu-speaking tribes arrived in the area, they brought livestock with them. These were a food reserve to tide them over lean times, but they also represented wealth for people who had limited opportunities for accumulating resources. In particular, stock animals were used as payments and gifts, leading to a complex web of social relationships, and the development of broader societies.

The veld in the Mapungubwe area is very dry at present, especially in winter. However, we are seeing it during a comparatively dry cycle and also at the end of a prolonged period of overgrazing by cattle owned by white farmers. Even still there is substantial grazing in the leaves and seeds of the widespread mopane. During the Mapungubwe period there would have been much more grass because of the higher rainfall.

Rocky Habitat and Rain-making

In the same way that walling and cultural remains are layered on top of each other, the rocks of the Mapungubwe area are of very different ages. The oldest are some of the most ancient rocks in the world, more than 3.5 billion years old. Slightly younger are the granite domes, such as at Klein Bolayi and Dongola Ranch next to the Musina road. Most of the area north of the Soutpansberg is the Limpopo Belt (see Appendix, page 232), which is over 2 billion years old.

The youngster in geological terms is the small patch of Karoo series sedimentary rocks in the Mapungubwe area, at only around 200 million years old. The 'caving sandstones' are the same as those making up Golden Gate, more than 600 kilometres to the south, and they also contain dinosaur fossils. They have eroded to create the interesting landscape so characteristic of the Mapungubwe area on the South African side, and small patches on the northern side of the river in Zimbabwe and Botswana.

From a cultural heritage perspective, these sandstones are important for two reasons. On the one hand, they have eroded to form caves that have been occupied for thousands of years by Stone Age San hunter-gatherers. On the other, they provide suitable inaccessible sites used by Bantu-speaking peoples for rain-making rituals.[4]

Ideal characteristics of these hills are steep sides with difficult access for cattle and natural cisterns or rock pools to store water. Excavations suggest that Mapungubwe Hill and Little Mapungubwe have been used for rain-making since about AD 600.[5]

Indian Ocean Trade

Trade across and around the Indian Ocean also receives very little attention in Eurocentric history books, which tend to focus on the Mediterranean and Atlantic trade. However, early writings by Arab travellers show that there has been ongoing trade up and down the coast of Africa, across to India and south-east Asia, and even directly across the ocean from Indonesia to Madagascar and on to Africa for many centuries.

It appears that round about AD 900 the traders sailing dhows extended their activities southwards to the first Sofala at the Bazaruto Islands, which was about as far as they could safely go without getting into the treacherous currents and winds of the present South African coast. These Arab traders were unlikely to have traded inland themselves, but would have had African intermediaries who would have traded directly overland to link up with the Limpopo River, and then up the river to Mapungubwe, and on into the interior.

The dhows brought glass beads, cotton and silk cloth, as well as ceramics. These were exchanged for ivory, leopard skins, copper, iron, and later gold from Zimbabwe. All transactions would have been heavily taxed, which would have gone directly to the Mapungubwe king, rapidly building up his wealth.

An interesting perspective is that the Venetian explorer, Marco Polo, was returning home from his visit to the Kublai Khan's empire, and introducing Europeans to the riches and culture of China, at the same time that Mapungubwe was at the height of its power, and receiving ceramics originating from China, as evidenced by the pot shards excavated at the site.

FOLLOWING SPREAD: Author Peter Norton gazes across the sandstone ridges and riverbed at dusk in much the same way that Jan Smuts may well have done as the beauty of this place is hugely captivating.

TOP: The park has excellent facilities for visitors starting at the main gate, as it is the only gate with the nearby cultural museum, depicting the area's ancient human history.

ABOVE: This abandoned building atop a ridge with magnificent views is reputed to have been one of the favourite spots of the former Prime Minister of South Africa, Jan Smuts.

LEFT: Peter Norton is dwarfed by one of the enormous trucks originally used to move coal from a nearby mine. Mining is a potential threat to biodiversity conservation and an increasing worry in water-scarce environments.

Why did the Mapungubwe Kingdom Collapse?

In Great Zimbabwe there are a number of theories on why the capital and the civilisation suddenly collapsed. In contrast, at Mapungubwe the abrupt end to the capital at around AD 1295 is very likely to be linked to the onset of what was called the Little Ice Age in Europe.

For a landscape that was probably close to its limit to produce sufficient food to feed all the people, just a small number of colder, drier years in a row would have been catastrophic. The colder weather would have shortened the growing season, and the lower rainfall would have caused crop failure both through direct rain on the soils, and through a breakdown in the flooding regime due to lower rainfall in the catchment areas.

There is evidence that people dispersed south and north-west, but it is not known what became of the royal family. Certainly there was a rapid increase at Great Zimbabwe around this time. It appears that the control of the trade, and the riches that this brought, moved directly to Zimbabwe, as well as the elite social structure and some of the customs. However, the pottery shows that the Zimbabwe leaders were mostly of a different group.

The location of Great Zimbabwe in the broader landscape of this part of southern Africa can also be related to the climatic changes. Whereas Mapungubwe is in the 'rain shadow' of the Soutpansberg for the prevailing rain-bearing winds that come from the south-east, and would therefore have been especially susceptible to climatic changes, Great Zimbabwe is ideally positioned on a south-east-facing slope to catch the rain winds, with no higher ground between it and the sea.

San Rock Art

The Limpopo River basin contains some of the richest rock art forms to be found anywhere in southern Africa with all four of the known types: San, Khoi, Iron Age farmer art and rock engravings.

The richness and splendour of these sites occurs in Zimbabwe, Botswana and the Limpopo Province amid the sandstone formations, and it extends to the Limpopo highlands (Waterberg) and the Makabeng range. Mapungubwe National Park and a number of private reserves actively protect these sites and they may be visited by arrangement. The newly opened magnificent Mapungubwe Cultural Museum is a must-visit to gain insight into the past history of the region. The husband and wife team, F and C Eastwood, who wrote *Capturing the Spoor*, is a work of great importance in our knowledge of these 'first people' on this astonishing landscape.

After Mapungubwe

The site that is now called Leokwe, 12 kilometres south-west of the confluence, was one of the main sub-capitals of the Mapungubwe kingdom. As you walk up the hill there are several sections of dry walling, still in good condition.

The myriad ruins in the Mapungubwe area are somewhat bewildering and confusing to the untrained eye. We found that the best way to interpret it was to think of layers upon layers of different ruins on top of one another. The ones that are likely to be most obvious are the more recent ruins, with the very old ruins being difficult to see unless they have been deliberately opened up for display. Most of the small and moveable artefacts have been removed to museums in Gauteng in any case.

The interpretation at Leokwe is that the earliest ruins were mostly no more than some indistinct hut circles at the base of the hill from the Zhizo period (when Schroda was the capital); and a few pot shards (fragments of clay pots) on top of the hill were from the Mapungubwe period; most of the walling is of a more recent Venda period, especially during the *difecane* period in the mid-1800s (when they may have needed to defend themselves from Mzilikazi's impis); and the 'loopholes' were inserted into more recently built, or re-built, walling from after the Europeans' arrival late in the nineteenth century.

One of the first waves of people after Mapungubwe was when the first Sotho-Tswana moved into the area from the north, during a warmer period around AD 1350. This was followed by several waves related to the collapse of Great Zimbabwe, from AD 1450 onwards, and the power struggles that followed, with Khami and Rozwi influences, occurring at various sites. Khami pottery and stonewalling show that Khami chiefs lived on Den Staat and near to Mapungubwe, although it seems that the area was rather sparsely populated. Later the valley was occupied by several groups of early Venda. The battles between different Venda groups, and then attacks by Mzilikazi's followers, led to the more jumbled defensive walling visible in places such as Bambandyanalo Hill above K2, Leokwe Hill and Mmamagwa Hill. However, there is a theory that the impact of Mzilikazi's Ndebele was actually quite limited in the Limpopo Valley.

Matshete, the name given to the farm to the south-west of Mapungubwe, was the dynastic title of one of the sons of the main Tshivula leader who lived near Salt Pan, and wanted a populated area close to the river as a buffer to invasion from the north. This leader actually lived on Leokwe Hill. The first Matshete, Raletupa, was

OPPOSITE: The river at its best when the flow is slow and lazy with only the sounds of birds at dawn.

LIMPOPO–SHASHE CONFLUENCE & MAPUNGUBWE   135

succeeded by Ranthsana, who was killed by a leopard. This unusual event led to accusations of witchcraft against Ranthsana's younger brother and uncle, both of whom were executed. This little story illustrates how the history of the people living along the Limpopo is richly entwined with the wildlife of the area.

Elephant hunting along this part of the Limpopo had been carried on since early times, and appears to have played an important part in the wealth of the area. Hunting of elephants seems to have escalated with the arrival of the white man. The first major hunter was legendary frontiersman Coenraad de Buys, who fled the Eastern Cape with his Xhosa wives and established a community of mixed 'Buysvolk' at Mara, just south of the Soutpansberg.

Buys's party was followed by Louis Trichardt's group of Voortrekkers, who stayed at Salt Pan for a while in 1836, before trekking on to Lourenço Marques (Maputo) where most of them died. Ten years later the area was more permanently settled with the establishment of Schoemansdal, close to Mara. It appears that Schoemansdal to a large extent owes its existence to the hunting of elephants. For example, in 1864 is it recorded that about 46 tonnes of ivory were exported from Schoemansdal, making up 85 per cent of the total export from the Transvaal. That is a lot of elephants to be hunted in one year. Explorer James Chapman reported that there were several Boers in the Soutpansberg area who claimed to have shot over 1 000 elephants.

After the upheavals of the Anglo-Boer War the state claimed all unsurveyed land in the Soutpansberg district, and several attempts were made to establish settlers there, interrupted by the ambitious Dongola Botanical Reserve (see box on page 124).

After World War II, and the deproclamation of the Dongola Wildlife Sanctuary, a number of forced removals took place, to ensure that the land was owned by the white settlers. In the early 1970s the South African Defence Force established a stronger presence in the area, and Greefswald, the farm on which Mapungubwe is located, became an army rehabilitation centre for drug addicts and alcoholics.

After the independence of Zimbabwe in 1982, the Limpopo was considered a key border area, and the camp was turned into an operational base, with the emblems of various units still preserved on the rocks at the confluence picnic site. It appears that some apartheid government cabinet ministers visited the area regularly, on the pretext of having bush breakaways. However, at least some of the attraction was for cabinet ministers and high-ranking officers to have private hunting at taxpayers' expense, sometimes even using military helicopters for this purpose!

OPPOSITE: The white rhino has been reintroduced into the areas surrounding and including the Mapungubwe National Park. Mapungubwe is particularly famous for rhino from San rock art paintings and 'The Golden Rhino'.

FOLLOWING SPREAD: Peter Norton beneath a magnificent baobab tree on an outcrop of sandstone on the banks of the river within the park.

Mapungubwe National Park

Two decades after the abortive Dongola Wildlife Sanctuary, the property Greefswald, on which Mapungubwe and K2 are situated, was proclaimed a provincial nature reserve by the administrator of the former Transvaal. Although it was ostensibly managed by the province, it remained a restricted area under SADF control, and no members of the public were allowed there.

In 1983 and 1984 the archaeological sites of K2 and Mapungubwe, respectively, were declared as national monuments under the old legislation. Then in 1995 the new Northern (now Limpopo) Province and the National Parks Board (now SANParks) agreed on the formation of a national park in the area, and the first property was proclaimed in 1998. Meanwhile, the declaration of a National Heritage Site and a World Heritage Site gathered momentum, and the Mapungubwe Cultural Landscape was listed in July 2003.

Because the various processes were happening simultaneously, the decision was taken to link the National Heritage Site, the World Heritage Site and the National Park together in such a way that as ongoing negotiations led to more properties being added to the national park, they would automatically be added to the heritage sites as well.

After an initial start as the Vhembe-Dongola National Park, the park was renamed the Mapungubwe National Park in 2004, a self-catering camp and picnic area and other facilities were provided, and the park was opened to the public. It is unusual among South African national parks in that it was primarily proclaimed because of its cultural value, with wildlife management and appreciation a secondary objective. In particular, the park aims to help visitors understand how various groups of people interacted with the landscape and the animals in it, which is a key theme for its World Heritage listing as a Cultural Landscape.

As one of the newest parks in the national parks family, Mapungubwe National Park is already attracting substantial numbers of visitors, most of whom are captivated by a visit to Mapungubwe Hill itself, the fascinating museum that outlines the history of the area, the Limpopo–Shashe confluence view site, the tree-top walk, the rock art sites, or merely spending time bird-watching, game-viewing or moving around in this mystical sandstone landscape.

OPPOSITE TOP: The south bank of the Limpopo has many fine examples of fever-trees within the national park. Mapungubwe is a park of many outstanding landscape features apart from its historical human presence.

OPPOSITE BOTTOM LEFT: The north side of the imposing Mapungubwe Hill, known as the 'place of many jackals' dating back to AD 800. There are a number of beautiful baobab trees at the base.

OPPOSITE BOTTOM RIGHT: A spectacular feature of the entire region is its trees, especially giant sycamore figs. This was the 'fig' of the ancients as far away as the Nile in Egypt.

Venetia Mine and Nature Reserve

As early as 1903 diamond gravels had been found on the farm Seta on the eastern end of Mapungubwe National Park. These were mined on and off for decades, but did not yield great riches. In 1969 De Beers Consolidated Mines, which originally developed at Kimberley, followed by Cullinan and other mines in South Africa, Botswana and Namibia, started a reconnaissance-sampling programme to locate the source of these river deposits. In this way they discovered, in 1980, the cluster of kimberlite pipes that now make up the Venetia Mine. After detailed feasibility studies, and shrewd buying up of suitable properties, the mine was opened in 1992, and is now the largest producer of diamonds in South Africa, with around five million carats extracted each year.

The process of separating diamonds from the crushed rock requires substantial amounts of water. Since the mine is just 25 kilometres south of the Limpopo River, it bought up more properties than were required for the mine itself, in order to obtain substantial water rights, and established a well-field in the Limpopo River, which pumps water to the Schroda storage dam, and on to the mine. Because of the shortage of water in this arid environment, the mine is also going to great lengths to save water and recycle as much as possible.

A further aim of obtaining the properties was to promote conservation in the area, and make a contribution to reviving the dream of the Dongola Wildlife Sanctuary, of which former De Beers Chairman Sir Ernest Oppenheimer had been a trustee in 1947. Several properties owned by De Beers have been incorporated into the Mapungubwe National Park, and south of the Park the 38 000-hectare Venetia Limpopo Nature Reserve has been established and managed by De Beers Farms Department. As an important buffer around the Mapungubwe National Park and World Heritage Site, Venetia Limpopo Nature Reserve will also from a part of the proposed Greater Mapungubwe Transfrontier Conservation Area. Already it is making a contribution to tourism in the area.

The Greater Mapungubwe Transfrontier Conservation Area (TFCA)

The Greater Mapungubwe TFCA is one of the two major TFCAs along the Limpopo River. As suggested in the box on page 124, the essence of the concept was first suggested by Jan Smuts more than 60 years ago, but it was immediately shot down for political reasons.

This TFCA was put forward as an integral part of the proposals for the Mapungubwe National Park and World Heritage Site around the turn of the millennium, and has been gradually worked on ever since. It is proposed to include the Mapungubwe National Park and World Heritage Site as the core, with the main buffer areas on the South African side being the privately owned Limpopo Valley Game Reserve, Venetia Limpopo Nature Reserve and Vhembe Game Reserve. On the Botswana side it will include Northern Tuli Game Reserve and the Tuli South Game Reserve, which is in the process of being developed. In Zimbabwe it is proposed to include Tuli Circle, Sentinel and Nottingham game reserves, as well as the proposed Maramani Reserve.

Largely due to Zimbabwe's political problems, progress has been slow, but it is gradually coming into being, and a Memorandum of Understanding was signed by the ministers from the three countries in June 2006. Already management of the game, particularly elephants, is being organised by staff on the ground, and discussions on coordinated management of cultural heritage resources is taking place. One of the key issues that will make the TFCA viable is coordinated tourism planning, with easy movement across borders, coordination of roads, bridges and airports, and packaging of the tourism product.

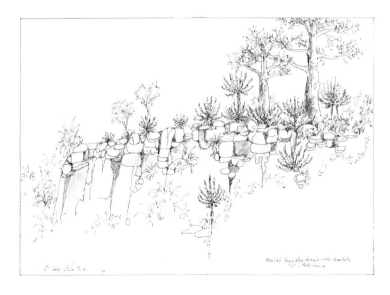

Mapungubwe area timeline

From 3000 BC
Occupation by San people.

450
First dated pottery of Bantu origin (Gokomere tradition) at Mapungubwe.

c. 900
Schroda is established as a major centre; the presence of ivory and beads is the first time that trade goods appear in the interior of southern Africa.

c. 1000
Abrupt change to Leopard's Kopje pottery suggests a possible 'invasion' from the south; Schroda is abandoned and the capital established at K2.

1400
Raphulu Dau arrive in Mapungubwe area from the West.

1450
Smaller groups from a declining Great Zimbabwe head south and occupy Limpopo Valley.

1652
Van Riebeeck lands at the Cape.

Early 1700s
Birwa and possibly Tlokwa chiefdoms colonise north and south of Limpopo.

1836
Voortrekker party under Louis Trichardt arrives in Zoutpansberg.

c. 1839
Mzilikazi's Ndebele move north from the Highveld through the area, but with limited impact on the local population.

1870
Elton launches his boat at the Limpopo–Shashe confluence looking for a navigable route to the sea.

1922
Dongola Botanical Reserve is established in the area.

1970s–80s
Area is occupied by the Defence Force as a Restricted Area.

1983/4
K2, Mapungubwe Hill and southern terraces are declared as National Monuments.

1995
The then Northern Province and National Parks Board agree on the formation of a National Park.

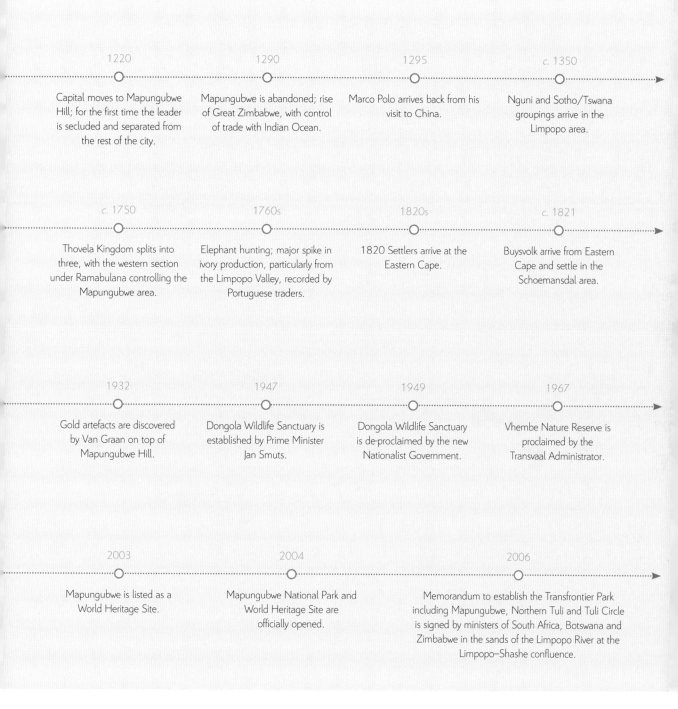

1220
Capital moves to Mapungubwe Hill; for the first time the leader is secluded and separated from the rest of the city.

1290
Mapungubwe is abandoned; rise of Great Zimbabwe, with control of trade with Indian Ocean.

1295
Marco Polo arrives back from his visit to China.

c. 1350
Nguni and Sotho/Tswana groupings arrive in the Limpopo area.

c. 1750
Thovela Kingdom splits into three, with the western section under Ramabulana controlling the Mapungubwe area.

1760s
Elephant hunting; major spike in ivory production, particularly from the Limpopo Valley, recorded by Portuguese traders.

1820s
1820 Settlers arrive at the Eastern Cape.

c. 1821
Buysvolk arrive from Eastern Cape and settle in the Schoemansdal area.

1932
Gold artefacts are discovered by Van Graan on top of Mapungubwe Hill.

1947
Dongola Wildlife Sanctuary is established by Prime Minister Jan Smuts.

1949
Dongola Wildlife Sanctuary is de-proclaimed by the new Nationalist Government.

1967
Vhembe Nature Reserve is proclaimed by the Transvaal Administrator.

2003
Mapungubwe is listed as a World Heritage Site.

2004
Mapungubwe National Park and World Heritage Site are officially opened.

2006
Memorandum to establish the Transfrontier Park including Mapungubwe, Northern Tuli and Tuli Circle is signed by ministers of South Africa, Botswana and Zimbabwe in the sands of the Limpopo River at the Limpopo–Shashe confluence.

CHAPTER 5

Dongola
to Crooks'
Corner

'Here along the Limpopo
I find the sweat and joy
of African adventure.'
– CAREL BIRKBY

Of Fugitives and Travellers

From Mapungubwe the river is relatively flat and meanders gently eastwards until close to Beit Bridge, with sufficient koppies on both sides of the river to keep the scenery changing. The fertile floodplains have mostly been cleared for irrigation lands and centre pivot systems, supporting crops such as citrus, cotton and tomatoes. This fate has befallen the beautiful forests on Weipe and Skutwater which were cleared some years ago. At the same time the river is cut off on the South African side by the ugly, formerly lethally electrified, Kaftan fence, which was erected to keep out insurgents as well as illegal immigrants. The riverine forest has therefore had the double blow of clearing for irrigation and then the wide, sterile swathe being cleared for the Kaftan fence, often through thick patches of forest. Nevertheless, it is possible to get onto the narrow tarred road along the fence without too many questions being asked, and this affords regular views of the river, particularly if one climbs some of the koppies right next to the road. On the northern, Zimbabwe side of the river the habitat is still in much better condition, with the attractive sandstone hills so typical of the Mapungubwe area stretching for 30 kilometres east of the Limpopo–Shashe confluence. Here are found the very attractive and culturally interesting private game farms of Sentinel and Nottingham.

Sentinel Ranch

Sentinel is a 32 000-hectare reserve that has been in the Bristow family for more than 50 years. Initially it was used for cattle farming, but this was never very successful, and the emphasis is now on safari hunting, with future potential for photographic tourism. Although constantly under threat of 'designation' and occupation by so-called 'war veterans' and/or army or police units, the ranch is still in excellent shape, and has good game populations. It is an obvious candidate to be part of the Limpopo–Shashe Transfrontier Conservation Area.

The farm starts opposite Schroda Dam in the Mapungubwe National Park, and has about 20 kilometres of Limpopo River frontage, with well-established riverine forest all along this length. There is a broad patch of pristine riverine and lala palm forest in an area protected from elephants that shows what the forest used to be like on the many kilometres of wide floodplain in this stretch of the river, before the irrigation lands were cleared.

OPPOSITE: These magnificent cliffs are located near the Kruger Park boundary and form part of the Madimbo Corridor – a beautiful and remote part of the river's eastward journey.

PREVIOUS SPREAD: Early morning mist rises over the Luvuvhu River in the northern Kruger National Park, home to large numbers of crocodile and hippo.

There is a wide variety of wildlife, and the remains of no less than 28 dinosaurs, from huge vegetarians to smaller carnivores, are found in the Karoo System rocks. One large five-metre *Massospondylus* has been partially excavated, providing an excellent example of how these fossils are preserved.

In addition to its great scenery and wildlife, Sentinel has a number of important cultural heritage attractions. So far 24 rock art sites have been identified, including an easily identifiable bottlenose fish, with a rare green outline, a scene with a herd of 14 elephants, and a saddle-billed stork. There are also several caves where locals used to store grain in large clay bins that are still intact. It is likely that these were emergency supplies kept out of sight of Mzilikazi's raiding parties. Large numbers of stone tools from the Middle and Late Stone Ages can be found, particularly in the caves, as well as the remains of several villages from Mapungubwe times, and fortified hilltops from the more turbulent Venda period.

From Sentinel, the gravel road on the Zimbabwe side goes through Nottingham, part of which is also being maintained as a game farm, and the Limpopo River floodplain has extensive irrigation lands. From here onwards the sandstone hills are left behind, and replaced once again by the more ancient granite koppies of the Limpopo Belt.

On the South African side, the road along the fence passes major irrigated agricultural lands. The majority of labourers on these farms are Zimbabweans, who are prepared to work for minimal wages – anything is better than what they could get in Zimbabwe at this stage. It suits the farmers who avoid South African unionised labour. The South African National Defence Force (SANDF) has identified this area, as well as Beit Bridge and Leeudraai near the Nzhelele confluence, as the main areas where illegal immigrants cross the border – in spite of the expensive and ecologically disruptive Kaftan fence. According to some sources the fence is not seen as an obstacle, since 'gomagomas' – the term for rather shady couriers – make a roaring trade guiding people across the border, sometimes even with their own keys to the gates. Every now and again the Zimbabwean police or army make a show of trying to stop the flow, but after a while things return to normal. SANDF units patrol the fence as a deterrent, but are more effective at picking up illegal immigrants at gathering points such as taxi ranks and shops away from the border.[1]

OPPOSITE: Young Eric Norton has an excellent view of the river road on the South African side of the border. The former 'lethal' electrified Kaftan fence originally erected to keep out insurgents crossing over from Zimbabwe can be seen.

BELOW: Great big baobabs dot this rugged landscape with the 'burning bush' creeper adorning the tree tops on the opposite bank of the river.

Edith Audrey Thompson, known to everybody as 'Googoo', was the wife of an English doctor, who lived most of her married life in the mountains around Magoebaskloof. In 1945 she went up to Messina (now known as Musina), ostensibly to say goodbye to all her friends after the war. However, her real reason was to go on an adventure she had dreamed of for years – to walk all on her own down the Limpopo to Pafuri! She needed a break from the farm and family obligations, but it was clearly an unusual approach for a woman of 50, particularly in those days!

Googoo's daughter, 'Box' Thompson, called her 'a silly old fool' for wanting to do the walk, but Googoo's response was, 'I want to get away from *everybody*. I want to do as *I* want to do. I want to walk when *I* want to walk; sleep and eat when *I* want to sleep and eat, and I *don't* want to talk to anybody.' In many ways this response gave a clue to Googoo's remarkably strong will, which had come to the fore in many other extraordinary adventures in remote parts of southern Africa.

Googoo's plan was to walk to her friend Tiny Mockford who lived with her husband, Harold, and their little daughter in the Witwatersrand Native Labour Association (WNLA) house at Pafuri. Harold's job was to process the steady stream of Mozambican residents who were on the way to the mines in the Witwatersrand.

Googoo advised the Chief of Police in Messina about her trip because, as she said, 'just after the war, all sorts of strange people were going through Beit Bridge to Rhodesia, and the authorities had to know that I was going into that wild country all on my own.' Googoo recalls that the response from the Chief of Police was similar to the response she had received from her daughter 'but couched in more polite terms!'

Her provisions consisted of two packets of raisins, a little bag of Tiger Oats, a packet of tea, some saccharine and a chunk of bread. For additional food she depended on the local people who, she hoped, 'would like some money for a bit of meat'. She had made a billycan out of a jam tin and she also took a big bathtowel, all of which was packed into her rucksack.

The first day found her about eight kilometres below Main Drift, and she camped next to a large dead leadwood tree. She took great care to wrap herself in her bathtowel and put her head inside her rucksack, for fear that a hyena might come and start eating her face. Her sleep was indeed interrupted by the visit of a hyena, but she chased it away. As she drifted back to sleep something touched her hair and she reacted quickly in case the hyena had returned. However, it turned out to be a large toad that must have come from under the log – this made her laugh and forget about the hyena.

At the Messina Company's farm, Doreen, she was approached by two 'Afrikaners' armed with rifles, who asked her what she was doing and told her she could not camp in the bush as it was not safe. They asked her if she was armed and, despite her assurance that she was not, they insisted that she empty her rucksack and show them her meagre rations. Apart from the food, she had a two-blade pocket-knife plus corkscrew, a tin opener and some personal items! Seemingly reassured by her harmlessness, she was left to sleep in the bush, and next morning she moved on.

On the third day she reached the house of Mr and Mrs Steenkamp who had already been told that Dr Thompson's wife was in the area, and that she was 'quite harmless'. Googoo did wonder, however, what words the Police Chief, Mr Evans, had used in describing her eccentric behaviour.

The fourth day of the walk brought her to 'a very difficult section of the river where the Limpopo runs under the rocks' and she had to jump from one rock to the next for about two miles (3.2 km). This was the gorge that had posed so much trouble for 'Brownie' Ramke and his friend Robertson in 1925 during their epic canoe trip from Messina towards the Indian Ocean.

Googoo recalled how she had ample time to observe and enjoy the animal and plant life and, on one occasion, she saw two Verreaux's eagles chasing baboons that had ventured too close to their nest. At the confluence of the Limpopo and the Bubye rivers that flowed in from the Zimbabwe side, she explored a graphite seam that was extracted by local potters to make the diamond shapes on their clay pots.

It was only towards the end of the walk that she started to see villagers from the area. At one spot she came across a group of local people who had killed a sable antelope. Thinking that she may be a policewoman in her loose khaki dress, felt hat and short-cropped hair, they scattered into the bush. 'The sable proved to be a welcome stroke of luck, because a few nice steaks cut off with my pocket-knife provided a good meal that evening!'

When she arrived at the Mockford's house after ten days and having covered approximately 84 miles (135 km), as the crow flies, she was not even hungry and recorded that 'nothing more terrifying had happened to me than the incident with those two Afrikaners who came after me with their rifles!'

Postscript: In spite of her adventurous attitude to life, or maybe because of it, Googoo Thompson lived to the ripe old age of 95, and died in her home near Haenertsburg in 1990.

Koppies and Engravings

Two koppies on the southern side of the river are of particular interest. Dongola Kop is a sandstone koppie that stands 400 metres above the river, 12 kilometres to the south, and dominates the landscape for kilometres around. Because of this it gave its name to the abortive Dongola Botanical Reserve of the mid-1900s (see box on page 124). The second is the rounded granite dome Klein Bolayi or Tshamavhudzi Rock, right next to the tarred road 20 kilometres before Musina. According to oral history, up to the 1800s weaker children such as albinos or the smaller of twins were killed by throwing them from the top of the rock.[3]

In Zimbabwe approximately 20 kilometres north of Beit Bridge and just west of the tarred main road after it crosses the Mtetengwe River (that flows into the Umzingwane) was a huge giraffe petroglyph. It was the intrepid Googoo Thompson (see box on page 152), who 'discovered' this rare rock engraving and brought it to the attention of the scientific world in the 1930s. She described it as 'a most beautiful and perfectly proportioned giraffe. Black moss had settled in the grooves, but the body markings, mane, tail and horns were perfectly outlined. It measured 9 feet [2.7 metres] from head to hoof'.[4] Today, there is no sign to mark its whereabouts and its present condition is unknown.

STEPHANUS CECIL RUTGERT
BARNARD

IN MEMORY OF   TER HERINNERING AAN
BVEKENYA
AND HIS WILD   EN SY TYDGENOTE
COMPANIONS WHO   OP DIE IVOORPAD
FOLLOWED THE
IVORY TRAIL
19 SEPTEMBER 1886 ~ 2 JUNE 1962

UNVEILED BY HIS SON
IZAK BARNARD
ON
19 SEPTEMBER 1986

TOP: Colin and Gary Norton at the Bvekenya Memorial. It was erected by the son, Isaac Barnard, and family in memory of Cecil 'Bvekenya' Barnard. He was the elusive and notorious elephant hunter from Crooks' Corner.

ABOVE: The crimson-red flowers of the 'burning bush' creeper, *Combretum microphyllum*, flower between August and November and are a feature of some of the best-preserved forests along the river.

LEFT: A close-up view of 'Bvekenya' Barnard's memorial, which is located in the Makuleke concession of the wild and beautiful northern Kruger National Park.

Umzingwane River and the Tolo-Azime Falls

The Umzingwane River enters the Limpopo approximately six kilometres upstream from Beit Bridge and drains a vast section of Zimbabwe's Matabeleland South Province. It was the centre of a major cattle farming industry up until the mid-1980s, before Zimbabwe's agricultural system collapsed. The enormous elephant in the Bulawayo Museum was shot on Doddieburn Ranch, an area that straddles the Umzingwane south of West Nicholson.

As one approaches Beit Bridge, the river becomes more and more rocky, and shortly after the confluence of the Umzingwane are the Tolo-Azime Falls where both Elton and Van Riet had narrow escapes during their boat trips (see pages 32 and 38. Elton apparently caused quite a stir in Victorian Britain when he described them to the Royal Geographical Society in 1872, 16 years after Livingstone had described the Victoria Falls. However, he reported the Tolo-Azime Falls to be as 75 feet high (22 metres), while Van Riet estimated them at only 20 feet (6 metres).

Since these two accounts there has been little mention of them, and the Musina Publicity Association had not even heard of them. We could only see them from the air, and not from the ground because the Kaftan fence cuts off this part of the river. They are unlikely to be anything of a tourist attraction until the Kaftan fence is removed, and access to the river restored.

Musina and Beit Bridge

Musina is South Africa's most northern town and is close to the Beit Bridge border post, the main road entry point into Zimbabwe. The town was founded on copper, rediscovered by prospectors early in the twentieth century. The whites called it Messina, but in the 1990s it was changed to the more correct name of Musina. The Musina people discovered and worked the copper in ancient times and it was called Musina, the 'spoiler', as it was considered to be a poor substitute for the iron that they were really seeking for their implements and weapons.

The commercial copper mine operated from 1905 until it formally closed in 1993, although various groups have been mining there for hundreds of years.

OPPOSITE TOP: The original Beit Bridge, which carries the pedestrian and rail traffic between South Africa and Zimbabwe.

OPPOSITE LEFT: Beit Bridge was named after Alfred Beit, a close friend of Cecil John Rhodes and one of the founders of Rand Mines Ltd.

OPPOSITE RIGHT: On the banks of the Limpopo a majestic baobab with reflection.

Approximately 10 kilometres south of the town is the entrance to the Musina Nature Reserve, previously known as the Messina Baobab Forest Reserve. An enormous number of baobab trees are protected within this reserve and visitors may also see various antelope. Also found within the reserve is one of the world's oldest datable rocks, a piece of granite gneiss that is 3 852 million years old.

The bridge crossing the Limpopo River is the Beit Bridge, named after Alfred Beit, who made his fortune as one of the pioneers of the diamond and gold mines in South Africa. He was a close colleague and admirer of Cecil John Rhodes, and one of the founders of Rand Mines Ltd. Beit Bridge was planned by Rhodes and Beit to be the first stage of what was to be their greatest memorial – the Cape to Cairo Railway. However, this grand imperial plan never came about.[5]

Today, the original Beit Bridge carries pedestrian traffic with the railway line linking South Africa to Zimbabwe next to it, and a new road bridge has been built immediately upstream of this old bridge. This is one of the main commercial routes up into Africa, and there are usually queues of large trucks waiting to cross the bridge and go through the border post.

About 15 kilometres east of Beit Bridge, shortly before the Sand River confluence, is the former Main Drift, which was used as one of the main entry points into Rhodesia (Zimbabwe) before the bridge was built. In 1891 it was the drift approached by the Banyailand Trekkers, a group of Boers who had been enticed to trek to northern Mashonaland close to the Zambezi by a contract with a chief that was supposedly independent of Rhodes's Charter. The British South Africa Company defended the border at several of the main drifts against the incursion, which would have undermined their Charter, with backing from the British Government. On crossing the river on reconnaissance, the leader of the Trekkers, Colonel Ignatius Ferreira, was arrested and brought before Dr Jameson, who 'persuaded' them of the pointlessness of their quest, which was also against President Paul Kruger's wishes.

Sand River

The Sand River enters the Limpopo 10 kilometres due east of the town of Musina. Its source is in the hills between Polokwane and Mokopane. Here it came to public attention when the Sandrivier railway siding close to the national road was the site of South Africa's Great Train Robbery in the 1980s. The source is also close to Eersteling, where gold was first mined and smelted by Edward Button in 1874.

North of Polokwane the river flows through a dreary landscape for almost 100 kilometres until it suddenly comes up against the Soutpansberg and has to find a way through. It does this through the dramatic 20-kilometre Waterpoort Gorge, which just has room for the river and the railway line to Musina. The Soutpansberg

TOP: Dr Sarah Venter points out lines of beautiful San rock art images of elephants on Sentinel Ranch on which there are 24 sites.

MIDDLE: The almost-complete remains of a 5-metre dinosaur, *Massospondilus*, has been partially excavated by natural elements from within the sandstone on Sentinel Ranch.

BOTTOM: Several sandstone caves have revealed the presence of well-preserved 'grain' bins hidden by the locals during the period of Mzilikase's reign of terror during the 1800s.

has great biological and cultural richness, and is one of 18 'centres of endemism' in southern Africa. One third of all known tree species in South Africa can be found in this range, as well as 76 per cent of South Africa's terrestrial and freshwater birds, 116 species of reptiles and amphibians, and 44 of the 50 fish species found in the Limpopo River System.

After the Sand River emerges from its impressive gorge, it flows across the baobab-studded plains leading down to the Limpopo River 10 kilometres east of Musina. From Musina there is a small public gravel road down to the Sand River confluence and along to Malala Drift.

Nzhelele River

The next river to enter the Limpopo downstream of the Sand is the Nzhelele. Legend has it that this was the point where the early migrants, the Balemba and the Basenzi (collectively known as the Singo) crossed the Limpopo from the north and then followed the river up into the foothills of the eastern Soutpansberg. They had been guided by their god, Mwalli, to leave their home in Zimbabwe in the early 1700s and travel south. Travelling with the Ngoma Lungundu, the great drum that had the power to cause thunder, hail and lightning, and confound any enemy that may stand against them, they moved up to the headwaters of the Nzhelele and established their capital at Dzata. In those far-off days the king was Thoho-ya-Ndou, the Head of the Elephant, and he wielded his power wisely to forge the many scattered tribes into one Venda nation. When Thohoyandou disappeared quite suddenly, it is reported that he took the Ngoma Lungundu with him and legend has it that they both disappeared into the waters of Lake Fundudzi, the Sacred Lake.

The Nzhelele River drains the hot springs at Tshipise, which is a well-known camping resort in this region. There are also several other hot springs, such as at Sagole Spa.

Nwanedi River

The Nwanedi and Luphephe rivers drain the northern slopes of the eastern Soutpansberg. Within the Nwanedi Nature Reserve both rivers are captured in the twin dams that provide a steady flow of water to the irrigation farms that lie between the reserve and the Limpopo.

OPPOSITE: The Limpopo basin has some of the finest examples of rock art of the San, Iron Age farmer art and that of the Khoe on the sandstone outcrops and overhangs.

As the Nwanedi flows towards the Limpopo it cuts through several sets of low hills with important cultural remains, particularly rock art, of which about 140 different sites have been identified. The Tshiugani Hills have ancient stone fortifications along the ridges. To the west lie the Ha-Tshirundu Hills and the privately owned Maremani Nature Reserve where big game and rock art sites are prime attractions. To the east are the Dambale Hills where caves and relics of recent cave dwellings can be seen. On the southern slopes of this range is the baobab of Sagole, one of the biggest trees of its kind in southern Africa.

Malala, Mohokwe and Qui-Qui Falls

Up to Malala Drift the river is very gentle, but from here onwards its nature changes. It becomes more turbulent and rocky as one enters what Van Riet[6] calls 'Limpopo Gorge', where the river drops 150 metres in 50 kilometres over a series of rapids and low waterfalls, to where it opens out at Mabiligwe just west of the Makuleke–Kruger Park boundary.

Madimbo Corridor

The Madimbo Corridor covers roughly the same stretch of the river as the Limpopo Gorge with the three waterfalls. It is situated all along the Limpopo River in a strip roughly five kilometres wide and 45 kilometres long, from Malala Drift in the west to the Makuleke–Kruger Park in the east.

As a border area the Madimbo Corridor is managed by the South African National Defence Force to control illegal activities, and is also used as a military training ground for infantry manoeuvres, parachute-jumping (see box on page 167), firing live rounds from rifles, mortars, canons, and air-to-ground missiles. Through the middle of the Corridor runs the Kaftan fence, which is supposed to serve the dual purpose of a veterinary fence to control foot-and-mouth disease and illegal human movements, especially immigrants and smugglers.

The Corridor is open to the river on the Limpopo side, and is often invaded by cattle from the multi-use livestock and wildlife area of Mtentengwe in Zimbabwe. The relatively undisturbed 51-kilometre stretch of riverine gallery forest is claimed to be the best example of this habitat in South Africa, and the Corridor has great biodiversity value, in addition to the dramatic scenery.

The Corridor was created in the 1960s to control infiltration of freedom fighters, forcibly removing a number of villages up to 10 kilometres to the south. After 1994 these villages have claimed the land under the Land Restitution Act and, after long delays, the land was granted to them in 2004. However, the exact terms under

which the Defence Force will lease the land back are still being sorted out. The most easterly parcel of land was handed back at an earlier date to the Shangaan villagers, who included it in the Makuleke region of Kruger Park. Unfortunately there has in the past been a small amount of not-very-profitable diamond mining close to the river – these are alluvial diamonds and not from a kimberlite pipe. People with mining interests have used this to raise huge expectations of numbers of jobs and wealth creation, and appear to have deliberately built up community resistance to what has by far the best chance of creating sustainable wealth – the tourism option making use of the dramatic scenery of the Limpopo Gorge and the position of the Corridor right next to the Kruger National Park.[7]

Bubye River

The Bubye flows in from the north and drains much of the southern Masvingo Province of Zimbabwe. A few kilometres upstream of the confluence are more hot springs that are used by the local people for washing and bathing. Near the confluence are bands of graphite, accessed by local pot-makers to decorate their clay pots. Just above the confluence is a village with the delightful name 'Chikwarakwara', referring to the sound made by the choruses of frogs in the wetlands alongside the rivers and streams.

FOLLOWING SPREAD: The bush-clad hills near Malala Hoek.

Makuleke/Crooks' Corner

At Mabiligwe on the southern side opposite Chikwarakwara the river enters the Makuleke section of the Kruger National Park, and the more recent sandstones of the Karoo System return. The first feature is Banyini Pan, with Mabyeni Kop next to it, which used to be part of the Madimbo Corridor, and was used as a DZ (Dropping Zone) for army parachutists (see box opposite).

Banyini Pan is the first of 31 seasonally flooded pans next to the Limpopo and Levuvhu rivers that make up the internationally recognised Limpopo/Luvuvhu floodplains and pans RAMSAR Wetland Site. In wet years they provide an important waterbird habitat during both summer and winter months, and serve as a stopover for many migratory waterbirds.[8]

Above the Manqeba wetland is a hill called Sesengambwe, which was the site of the Makuleke Store built in 1910 by Alex Thompson and William Pye, and used as a base by 'Bvekenya' Barnard and many of the other rough-and-ready characters that gave the area the name of Crooks' Corner (see box on page 174). After passing through the hands of several different owners and managers, it was run for nine years by 'Buck' Buchanan, a character in his own right, of American-Canadian origin who landed up in this neglected corner of South Africa and took a local wife. In Buck Buchanan's days the land between the Luvuvhu and the Limpopo was not known as Crooks' Corner, but he and the others were known collectively as 'Ali Baba and the Forty Thieves'. It is said that the Sergeant d'Arcy, in charge of the first police post in Sibasa established in 1910, often wrote letters to Buck Buchanan and asked him, 'How is it going with the other thirty-nine?!'

A few kilometres further on are the lonely graves of Hendrik Hartman and William Pye, and further to the south the memorial to Bvekenya Barnard close to 'Buck Buchanan's Baobab'. Near Crooks' Corner itself are the remains of John Fernandez's store, which was used right up to 1950, and a kilometre further on the confluence with the Luvuvhu River, which marks the three-way border split between South Africa, Zimbabwe and Mozambique.

Peter Norton's army parachute jump at Banyini Pan

In 1971, as a young 'parabat' during his year of compulsory military service, Peter Norton jumped out of a large transport aeroplane at Banyini Pan, to go on army training manoeuvres in the Madimbo area. Here are extracts from his diary kept at the time.[9]

'Tension rose as the large cargo door of the "flossie" lowered, and the rushing air brought in the smell of the dry Limpopo bushveld. We dropped a cargo chute over the drop zone, and watched it float gently to the ground 300 metres below. Cargo door up and open parachute doors as we circled round for our long run in. My eyes focussed intently on the red light above the head of the sergeant in front of me.

'"Stand in the door!!" … green light. "Go!!" The sergeant vanished in front of me as I shuffled awkwardly forward into the door, with my 40 kg kit (full kit, rifle and large radio) strapped to my leg. "Go!!" A hard thump on my shoulder, as I looked straight ahead and jumped. Zzzippp! and the wind whisked me away. Suddenly it was quiet … the roaring of the engines and the rushing of the wind was gone.

'A violent tug on the harness as I looked up and watched the beautiful green canopy unfold above me (it looks very beautiful when your life depends on it!). I looked down to check there was nobody below me, and released the catches to drop my kit, so that it could swing on the end of a 5 metre rope and hit the ground first, thereby slowing my fall at the critical moment before I hit the ground.

'Still quite a way to go … I had time to look around me and enjoy the view. Above and to my right the rest of the stick hung in the air like a line of green mushrooms against the morning sky. But what a sight below! In front of me a large rocky koppie (later identified as Mabyeni), and next to it the wide sandy Limpopo riverbed forming an arc into the distance. On both sides the bushveld that we have been looking forward to …

'Suddenly the yellowing reeds of the pan below started to rush up at me … watch out for those fever-trees! … OK, we're well clear. "Dooff!" as my kit hit the ground, and a sudden lump in my throat … Crash!! – a terrible landing, but I was OK. Out with the camera, and my hands were still shaking when I took pictures as the next plane flew over and the sky was full of green mushrooms again. One of my buddies landed almost on top of me …'

This was the beginning of some of the happiest weeks during his year of military service. Apart from the usual 'playing soldiers', his diaries talk of watching the sunset from Mabyeni Koppie, fishing in the pools in the Limpopo, looking for game from the Alouette helicopters (supposedly practising manoeuvres!), bird choruses in the morning, driving through the bush tracks in the chilling morning air, and sunset strolls up the sandy riverbed. This was a period that built a lifelong relationship with the bushveld in general, and the Limpopo River in particular.

ABOVE: Towards the border post of Beit Bridge along the road that runs parallel to the river on the Zimbabwean side, one is likely to encounter locals and, on occasion, so-called former 'war' vets, police and army units going about their daily business.

OPPOSITE: A length of protected Ilala palm and riverine forest on Sentinel Ranch well illustrates the absence of large numbers of elephant along this stretch of the river. Further south upstream of the Zimbabwean border post the riverine forest is also in pristine condition.

Chief Makuleke and the Deku Meeting Tree[10]

'Deku, Deku' the tribal police called out as they ran from village to village summoning the headmen and elders to a meeting with the chief under the *Nhelengeletano* (Shangaan for 'meeting') baobab at Deku.

Deku was the name of an old lady, one of the first settlers in the Makuleke area in the mid-1800s, when the Shangaans of the Gaza Kingdom moved northwards under pressure from Swazi and Zulu raiders in the south. She later died under a baobab tree, and from then onwards the site was known as Deku.

The gathered headmen from the seven villages bowed down as the tall and resolute Chief Makuleke walked through them to take his seat on the special wooden chair covered with a leopard skin that had been placed on the slightly higher ground among the roots of the baobab. The headmen and elders sat on the ground, so that the chief was slightly above them – having their heads higher than his would be disrespectful.

Each headman was expected to report on activities and problems in his village, and to discuss important issues affecting the tribe. However, on this occasion these reports were overshadowed by a much more urgent topic, the planned forced removals of the tribe by the hated apartheid government, so that their land could be included in the Kruger National Park.

One by one the elders and headmen brought up a number of issues:

'We have been here for a hundred years, and our ancestors are buried here. Will we have access to their graves?'

Luvuvhu and Mutale Rivers

The Luvuvhu enters the Limpopo at Crooks' Corner. While the Limpopo is usually 'dry' outside of the wet season, the Luvuvhu carries water all year round, and the banks are alive with crocodiles.

The Luvuvhu River brings a wealth of history, mystery and legend to the waters of the Limpopo. It rises close to the town of Makhado and its flow is temporarily held up by the Albasini Dam, north-east of the historic Elim Hospital.

The Albasini Dam is named after one of the most colourful characters of the nineteenth century, João Albasini, who came to the area as the officially elected chief of the 'Knopneuse' – the Magwamba section of the Shangaan tribe. At the same time he was a Justice of the Peace for the area and the Portuguese Vice-Consul in the Transvaal. João, his wife and several family members are buried close to the recreation resort on Albasini Dam.

Below the dam, the river flows through tropical fruit orchards and Venda villages and passes close to Tshimbupfe where the remains of old iron furnaces may still

'Our women make baskets to trap fish in the floodplains of the Luvuvhu and Limpopo rivers. This is an important source of food for us. But there are no big rivers where they want to take us.'

'Will there be the wild animals that we have been hunting for meat for many years?'

'How will we make *uchema* [a tasty and nutritional wine] if there are no lala palms?'

'This place is rich in fruits and nuts to keep our children strong and healthy.'

'The traditional healers will not have the diversity of berries and roots and leaves to heal our sickness.'

'Will there be the tasty *mashonzha* [mopane worms] in mid-summer that we can collect and dry to keep us through the winter?'

'We need the hard *nsimbitsi* [Lebombo ironwood] trees to build our houses, because they are resistant to termites. These only occur in Makuleke and the Lebombo mountains.'

It was clear that this rich and diverse area between the Luvuvhu and Limpopo rivers fulfilled many of the needs of the Makuleke people, and the meeting resolved to stand fast in their ancestral lands.

Chief Makuleke and his people strongly resisted being forcibly removed from 1939, when it was first gazetted, until Chief Makuleke's death in 1967. Then the transitional leadership situation was exploited by the Nationalist government, and in 1969 the people were forced, at gunpoint, to burn their own homes and be transported to a site south of Punda Maria. The remains of the chief's village can be seen just over the hill from the Deku tree, as well as at several other sites in the Makuleke area.

be seen. Tshimbupfe was an important centre of iron mining and iron implement and weapon production in days gone by and some of the major trade routes passed through this point. The Lwamondo Hill looks down on the Luvuvhu from a distance and it was here that a troop of baboons once warned the local villagers of approaching danger. To this day, the baboons are respected and protected.

Just east of the Kruger Park's Punda Maria Gate, the Luvuvhu becomes the border between the Kruger Park and the adjoining Makuya Park. This is wild, beautiful and remote country and old stonewall fortresses look down on the gorge that snakes its way ever closer to the Limpopo. As the gorge broadens out, the Luvuvhu is joined by the Mutale, probably the most revered of all rivers in Venda.

The Mutale rises in the plantations and forests of Thate Vondo, and is one of three rivers that flow into Lake Fundudzi, South Africa's only true natural inland lake, which was created by a landslide. It has special significance for the Singo people in that they believe their ancestral god lives within its waters. Lake Fundudzi is a truly magical place and is the home of many legends.

Water spirits are said to inhabit the lake in a friendly relationship with the python – a symbol of fertility and creation and closely associated with the '*domba*' initiation dance – and the white crocodile that requires that various first-fruit sacrifices are made. However, there is rising concern that the long-term survival of the lake is threatened by siltation from unwise and unsustainable land-use practices within the catchment.

The Mutale River passes through a magnificent 30-kilometre-long gorge that extends from the villages of Tshikundamalema to Guyuni, and when the river is flowing strongly, this gorge offers some of South Africa's finest Grade Five rapids for white-water canoeists and rafters. Shortly before entering the Luvuvhu, the Mutale plunges into a series of spectacular potholes. Tiger fish are to be found in this stretch of the river and, subject to securing an official licence, they offer excellent angling opportunities.

The combined waters of the Mutale and the Luvuvhu flow through the spectacular Lanner Gorge and on past the Thulamela archaeological site high up on the hills south of the river (see opposite box). The Luvuvhu is the southern boundary of the Makuleke concession that extends up to the Limpopo and is home to much rich history and natural splendour.

Thulamela

The young black SANParks ranger relaxed on a rock on the edge of a cliff overlooking the valley that had once been the fields of Thulamela, the home of his ancestors. In his hands he cradled a rifle, to guard visitors to the site from wild animals, in much the same way that a young bodyguard of the king would have sat five-and-a-half centuries ago, cradling his spear to keep a look-out and protect the king from his enemies.

There is an eerie stillness and an aura of mystery that surrounds these ancient walls on a hill overlooking the Luvuvhu and Limpopo valleys and surrounded by some huge old baobab trees. The Thulamela people left Zimbabwe after the collapse of Great Zimbabwe, heading south in about 1450, and establishing a number of chieftaincies of roughly equal status along the Limpopo Valley.

Unlike Mapungubwe, which is too far back, Thulamela can be directly linked to the Venda of today. Excavations at the site revealed the grave of an old king. Once archaeological information had been collected, his bones were respectfully reburied in a moving ceremony that showed the Makahane people acknowledging their long-gone ancestors.

The walls of Thulamela have been largely re-built and, to date, it represents the oldest restored buildings in South Africa. Excavations have revealed gold bracelets and beads, ivory amulets, clay pots from the Khami era, glass and shell beads, harpoons, spearheads and ceramic spindle whorls. Of particular importance was the discovery of the grave of a lady of high estate. She was found lying on her side in the 'Losha' position, showing respect, with her hands on the left side of her face, and with a beautiful gold bracelet around her arm. She was nicknamed 'Queen Losha' by the excavation team.

The layout of the capital reflects the pattern of Ritual Seclusion of the Sacred Leader that started at Mapungubwe, and carried on through Great Zimbabwe. One of the young bodyguards' jobs would be to ensure that no commoners gained access to the king or the Makhadze, his ritual sister, who ruled with him.

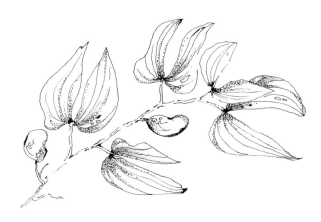

Cecil Barnard or 'Bvekenya' (Shangaan meaning 'the one who swaggers when he walks') was one of the colourful, rough, but interesting characters who epitomise the 'bad old days' of Crooks' Corner.

Bvekenya was born in Knysna in 1886 of cosmopolitan parentage with a father of Scots descent and a mother of Dutch-Irish origin. He had a tough youth. Soon after moving to the South African Republic, they lost all but three of their 300 cattle in the rinderpest epidemic of 1896–97. During the Anglo-Boer War, Barnard's father fought for the Boers, and was soon captured, leaving his mother and himself, as the oldest of five children, to manage the farm as best they could. His mother soon died, leaving 15-year-old Cecil to look after his four younger brothers and sisters until his father returned at the end of the war. Suddenly he was free to do as he chose.

With little education, no money and no connections, but good health, toughness and patience, he set out into the world. After three years of discipline in the new South African Constabulary, his boyhood dreams of a carefree life hunting elephants in the wilderness drew him to the Pafuri region, soon to become known as Crooks' Corner.

When he first arrived there in 1910 in his newly purchased donkey wagon, Bvekenya was dressed rather like a cowboy, causing much amusement to the locals. Alec Thompson, who managed the new Makuleke store, was hospitable but unenthusiastic about yet another story of the fortune to be made in elephant hunting.

Bvekenya's first hunting expedition in Mozambique (then known as Portuguese East Africa) was a disaster because he was set upon by a group of Shangaans, led by a police sergeant, and robbed of everything, including most of his clothes. He escaped by swimming across the river, but still had 250 kilometres to walk, barefoot, back to Makuleke, during which he was helped by a group of returning mineworkers. He trekked back to Pretoria, found it stifling and, against all advice, decided to continue with his dream.

One of his first tasks was to repay the debt to the returning mineworkers who had helped him after the Sabi attack. When he reached their village north of the Sabi River he found all its inhabitants on the verge of death from starvation. Bvekenya immediately hunted some game and spent several weeks there nursing the villagers back to health. This gesture, together with many later acts of kindness, made him loyal friends who were to prove very useful in informing him of police anti-poaching patrols and, later, with recruiting mineworkers.

This reputation for kindness was counterbalanced by a fearsome treatment of those who crossed him. After building up his resources by poaching several elephants, Bvekenya avenged

his attack on the Sabi. Apart from the leader, whose eye he had put out during the fight, he patiently gathered information on the other participants and sought out their villages. He set the buildings alight and personally thrashed his previous attackers, in a standard routine that was to become famous as his 'culture of the bush'.

Bvekenya built up experience to become a skilful elephant hunter, and he poached hundreds over a period of nearly 20 years, in the wide area from the Sabi Valley down to the Limpopo and the border with the Kruger National Park. He showed little regard for the authorities whom he always evaded based on tip-offs from his network of informants.

Bvekenya used the Makuleke store as his main source of supplies, and the rich characters who lived in the area were his source of social contact. For a long time his camp was several kilometres away on an island in the middle of the Limpopo River (which has now been washed away by the floods), where the three-way boundary between Mozambique, Zimbabwe and South Africa was marked by a large beacon. The area had developed a reputation as Crooks' Corner, because its inhabitants could evade capture by slipping across to a neighbouring country, but Bvekenya took this to a new level. After tiring of moving his camp around the beacon to evade whichever country's police patrol was looking for him at the time, he prised the beacon loose, and found it a whole lot easier to move the beacon round his camp!

Bvekenya was a trusting friend to some of the characters in Crooks' Corner, and took much trouble in nursing them back to health during bouts of malaria or blackwater fever, or from hunting injuries. In contrast, a Swede called Colsen from a rival recruiting syndicate, who was accused by Barnard of abducting recruits, was chased away from Crooks' Corner by a 'Barnard uppercut punch'.

Much of the police's interest in him was based on his reputation rather than hard evidence, and he eventually managed to clear his name with the South African police. After working with a private syndicate to recruit mine labour, he was employed by Witwatersrand Native Labour Association (WNLA) for a while, using his extensive knowledge of the area and strong network of informants. However, he did not fit comfortably into a structured organisation, and went back to poaching elephants.

One of the last elephants he pursued was Dhlulamithi, a huge '100-pounder' tusker that he had seen years before. According to his account recorded in TV Bulpin's book *The Ivory Trail*, he actually caught up with Dhlulamithi and lined up for a shot, but was overcome with emotion and respect and decided to leave the mighty elephant alone. Shortly afterwards he left Crooks' Corner and went to farm in the Western Transvaal. Most of the furniture in his farmhouse was made of mahogany, and his fence posts of Lebombo ironwood, all cut in the Crooks' Corner area.

ABOVE: Looking across the river one sees one of two prominent sandstone outcrops, the 400-metre-high Dongola Kop after which the original Dongola Botanical Reserve was named.

The Makuleke Story

As shown in the box on page 170, in 1969 the Makuleke tribe were forcibly removed from their land, which formed a triangle between the Luvuvhu and Limpopo rivers. While conservationists were jubilant at what seemed a logical addition to the Kruger National Park, most of us were unaware of the heartbreak it had caused, and the poor conditions that the Makulekes had been moved to.

Following the election of the new government in a Democratic South Africa in 1994, the Makulekes reclaimed their land under the new Land Restitution Act. Their claim made history as one of the first to be recognised in the New South Africa. It involved the Makulekes obtaining full title to their ancestral land based on an agreement whereby they guaranteed to use it in a way that is compatible with wildlife conservation. They agreed not to occupy, farm or mine the land, but gained full rights to commercialise it by entering into partnerships with private investors to build game lodges and camps as long as these were consistent with the wildlife management policies of SANParks. In terms of the agreement, the area must be managed by a Joint Management Board which empowers the community to manage the land themselves within the broad conservation guidelines.

The arrangement provides a role model of how the protection of biological diversity can be harmonised with the interests of local people who were excluded from the benefits of conservation for most of the last century. In terms of the agreement, about 24 000 hectares was de-proclaimed and returned to the community, but then immediately re-proclaimed as a contractual park, effectively reincorporating it back into the Park and under the overall management system. To show that the community is serious about developing the area as a conservation-based tourism destination, they added another 5 000 hectares of their communal land to the Park. So this means that the Park has actually increased, rather than reduced, due to the land claim.

A key part of the development is that a formal structure has been created. The community is represented by a Community Property Association which is legally empowered to negotiate with the conservation agencies and with tourism investors and operators. This is a hybrid between the traditional and new democratic type of organisation, since the present Chief Makuleke sits on the board *ex officio*, and therefore has a substantial say in how business is carried out.

The other key development is that of partnerships with aid agencies and with the private sector, both as advisors to help build capacity in the association, and as developers and operators in tourism. Already R60 million has been mobilised for investment in tourism; two major upmarket lodges, the Outpost and Pafuri Camp of Wilderness Safaris are fully operational, annually yielding several million rand in revenue for the Makuleke community.

In addition, there have been major training, capacity-building and job-creation spin-offs. At a higher level, the Makuleke leadership have had formal training and learned much about operating in a commercial world. Field rangers have been trained and are responsible for the management of the area. In the lodges, as part of the concession, the majority of staff have to be Makuleke.

The area is a model for community involvement in tourism and conservation, and proves that, in the right situation, wildlife-based tourism in a properly declared and managed conservation area can yield the better returns for communities than farming and grazing of cattle.

Timeline for the Dongola to Crooks' Corner section

Mid-1400s	1690s	Mid-1800s	1896–7
After the break-up of Great Zimbabwe, a Lembethu group crosses the Limpopo and builds Thulamela.	Singo group breaks away from Rozvis, crosses Limpopo River and moves up Nzhelele River to establish a capital at Dzata and mould various groups into the Venda nation.	Ancestors of the Shangaan Makuleke tribe settle in the triangle between the Limpopo and Luvuvhu rivers; Elton's boat trip down the river from the Shashe confluence to Tolo-Azime.	Rinderpest epidemic decimates game populations in the Lowveld; Musina commercial copper mine is established; Makuleke Store is built, and Bvekenya Barnard moves to Crooks' Corner; WNLA is established to formalise recruiting of labour for the mines.

ABOVE: Visitors to Crooks' Corner take time out for sundowners in the dry Limpopo River.

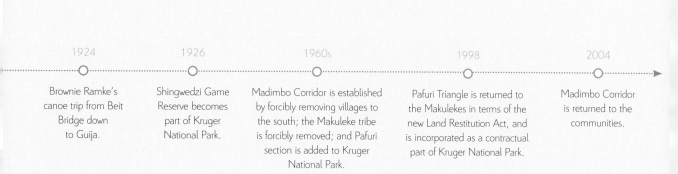

1924	1926	1960s	1998	2004
Brownie Ramke's canoe trip from Beit Bridge down to Guija.	Shingwedzi Game Reserve becomes part of Kruger National Park.	Madimbo Corridor is established by forcibly removing villages to the south; the Makuleke tribe is forcibly removed; and Pafuri section is added to Kruger National Park.	Pafuri Triangle is returned to the Makulekes in terms of the new Land Restitution Act, and is incorporated as a contractual part of Kruger National Park.	Madimbo Corridor is returned to the communities.

Paul Neergaard, Harold Mockford and the 'Wenela' Station at Pafuri[12]

Paul Neergaard was a tall Norwegian who was an excellent horseman and loved walking and studying birds. He was also the first regional manager of the Witwatersrand Native Labour Association (WNLA; commonly known as 'Wenela'). It was set up to organise and control the recruitment of locals in Mozambique, Rhodesia (now Zimbabwe) and further north to work as labourers on the mines many kilometres to the south on the Witwatersrand. The most important route for these recruits was through the Wenela Station at Pafuri, close to the confluence of the Limpopo and Luvuvhu rivers.

Before Neergaard's appointment in 1918, recruiting of labour was done on a more informal basis by 'blackbirders', many of whom were based in Crooks' Corner, and one of the best known being Bvekenya Barnard (see box on page 174). In those bad old days there was much skulduggery, with serious fights breaking out over 'stealing' one another's recruits. And the people who often lost out the most were the recruits themselves. When WNLA 'cleaned up the act', Paul Neergaard actually recruited Bvekenya to work for them for a while, but he only lasted for a few years.

For the first three years Paul Neergaard was based at Pafuri, and organised the setting up of the camp there. The system worked as follows: prospective labourers were recruited deep in the bush in Mozambique and given a blanket and basic clothing; they walked in gangs along well-known paths (often the centuries-old trading routes) to the Limpopo; they would then deal with any border formalities required (very few in Neergaard's time, but quite complicated later), stop over at Pafuri, and then continue through to Soekmekaar on the railway line, 240 kilometres to the south.

They travelled up to 25 kilometres per day, so there had to be organised camps at these intervals, to provide them with food, and to protect the pack animals (mostly donkeys) that carried their few possessions. Each of these camps had to be near water, although for some the provision of water was an ongoing battle. On the South African side near the Limpopo River, the stopovers were at Pafuri itself, Klopperfontein, and Shikokololo, which later became Punda Maria Rest Camp in the Kruger National Park. Later an additional outpost was established at a fountain close to the conspicuous Baobab Hill between Pafuri and Klopperfontein. These outposts were the same as those used by Bvekenya and other visitors to Crooks' Corner in the early days.

The original buildings at Pafuri were made of 'wattle and daub', using the very strong and termite-resistant Lebombo ironwood of the area.

From the beginning close cooperation was established between the WNLA staff and the managers of the Shingwedzi Game Reserve, which became the Kruger National Park in 1926. WNLA played a major role in opening up the

country, first with just footpaths, but later in the construction and maintenance of roads, both on the South African side and in Mozambique. In fact this part of Mozambique would probably have taken many more decades to be opened up to motorised transport if it were not for the huge investment by WNLA.

Paul Neergaard spent three years at Pafuri, after which he moved to Soekmekaar, the main base on the railway line. During a three-month reconnaissance expedition to the north of the Save River, Neergaard contracted such a serious bout of malaria that he only just survived and had to go on pension due to ill health.

After several interim managers at Pafuri, Harold Mockford was appointed, and remained there for the record period of 47 years until his retirement in 1985.

Although motorised transport of recruits in buses had started in 1928, the roads were still in terrible shape when Mockford arrived in 1938. He reported that a bus trip from Pafuri to Soekmekaar in 1938 took a full week to cover the distance of 240 kilometres. In comparison, one can now travel the distance in just over three hours on tarred roads, and it would be even quicker were it not for the speed restrictions for the last section within the Kruger National Park.

The Limpopo River was used by WNLA all the time. At several crossings of the river in Mozambique, large flat-bottomed boats were stationed to transport the recruits across during floods. During high floods these boatmen often played an important role in rescuing locals trapped on islands or in trees, and these brave actions were seldom recognised. Their main compensation was that domestic and wild animals that had drowned in the floods could be reached, and this provided a welcome supply of meat. At the end of the wet season, strips of gravel were laid over the river sands, and these were covered with reeds, so that the buses could cross during the dry months.

Largely due to Mockford's willingness to organise things and take on extra responsibilities (he was a part-time customs and immigration officer for 22 years, and a National Parks Board honorary ranger for many years), the stream of mine recruits continued throughout World War II. The number grew to 22 000 recruits in 1975, but after this the Frelimo takeover in Mozambique resulted in unscrupulous officials being stationed in this remote part, and relations deteriorated so much that the gate was eventually closed.

During this period WNLA also became TEBA, The Employment Bureau of Africa Ltd, but the organisation is still referred to using its old name by people who fondly remember the contribution that it made by opening up this remote part of Mozambique, and of course the South African Lowveld.

FOLLOWING SPREAD: Beautiful sandstone outcrops and baobabs dot the Sentinel Ranch landscape.

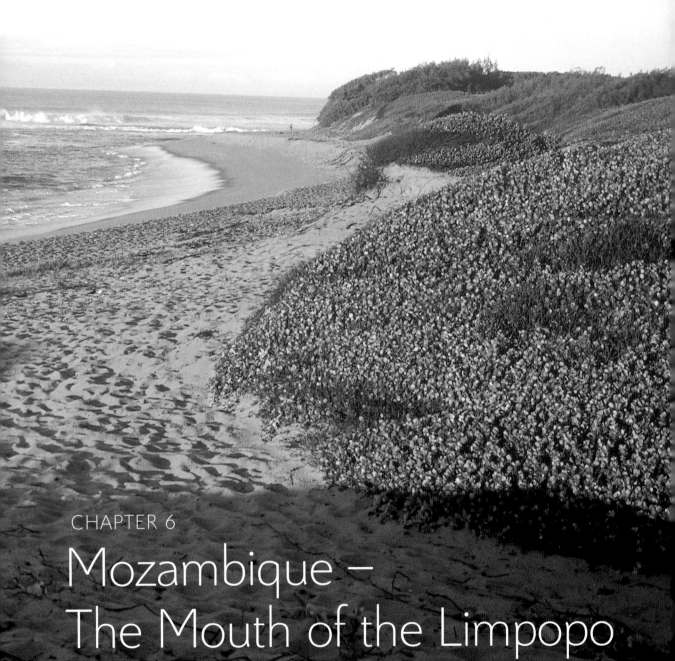

CHAPTER 6

Mozambique –
The Mouth of the Limpopo

'A few moments after, I stood
gazing on the long-sought
mouth of the Limpopo or
Bembe River.'

– St Vincent Erskine

Journey's End

Pafuri to Mapai

Three kilometres south of the three-way border split at Crooks' Corner is the remote Pafuri Border Post into Mozambique, nestled among the fever-trees. This was quite busy in the WNLA days (see box on page 180) when it was used as the main entry point for aspirant and returning miners on their way to the Witwatersrand. Now the border traffic is more of a trickle, with 4x4s from South Africa heading out on an adventure, as well as a few Mozambicans. Some of these are people with vehicles living in the far inland areas who find it convenient to use the better roads on the South African side to get to Maputo.

Immediately the landscape takes on the character of rural Mozambique, with generally run-down buildings and lots of locals sitting in the shade, some of them selling clothes or basic foodstuff.

From here on the river is very flat – at Pafuri it is only 200 metres above sea level, with more than 400 kilometres to go to the sea. The river is surrounded by rolling hills, many with thatched houses on top, and the road wends its way through dry pans that are obviously waterlogged in the rainy season. These pans are part of the same system that has been declared a RAMSAR site on the South African side, and are reported to have many waterbirds during good rain years.

The gravel road to Mapai is of a fairly good standard, at least in relation to what lies ahead, and good progress can be made. It passes through many villages, interspersed with cleared lands. There are lots of trees, but the grass is heavily grazed by the many multi-coloured Nguni cattle, as well as the omnipresent goats. After about 20 kilometres, the twin power lines of the Cahora Bassa line cross the river

OPPOSITE: Golden light at sunset bathes the ground on a high bank of the river in the Northern Tuli Game Reserve.

PREVIOUS SPREAD: The Limpopo River Mouth, first sighted and recorded by the Portuguese navigator, Vasco da Gama in 1498 when, together with three ships under his command, he anchored at its mouth.

from up north, and carry power across the Kruger National Park into South Africa.

The road is generally a few kilometres from the river, and only provides occasional glimpses of the Limpopo weaving its way through the fever-trees, with baobabs dotted around, mostly on the hills. Unfortunately the confluence with the Nuanedzi (or Mwenezi as it is called in Mozambique) is out of sight in the distance.

Just before Mapai is the site of the proposed new Mapai Dam, a major irrigation dam that would push back for some distance up the river. It is not clear whether it is really viable or not, because there would be a major problem with siltation from all the silt coming down the Limpopo during floods, and in any case the soils in this part of the river are not nearly as good as below Matsambo, and the floodplain is far narrower. What is obvious, though, is that it would substantially change the lifestyles of the people living in this remote and forgotten part of Africa, and put serious pressure on the new Limpopo National Park.

BELOW: The rather drab-looking Pafuri Border Post on the Mozambique side welcomes travellers to what may well be a most interesting journey if one sticks to the west bank of the Limpopo River.

OPPOSITE: A strange but interesting baobab, with what appears to be a door cut into it, lies alongside the gravel road to Mapai. Many of these trees may be seen dotting the ridges along the route.

ABOVE: The river crossing to the town of Mapai some 80 km from the Pafuri Border Post.

Mapai

After about 80 kilometres our route reaches a store at Chicumbane, and then the main track goes down to cross the river to Mapai. There is no bridge or crossing structure – when the water is low, you simply drive across the sand and through any puddles that may be left. But when the level is higher, it is a more adventurous deep-water crossing for vehicles. Even then, the water flows slowly, and we watched the local people carefully walk through the chest-high water, balancing their goods on their heads to join up with transport on the other side.

From the crossing the track works its way up the small escarpment to the town of Mapai (also shown as São Jorge do Limpopo on some maps), which has a railway station on the Chicualacuala line up to Zimbabwe, and used to be an important base for insurgents moving into Rhodesia (as it was then) during the '60s and '70s Bush War. Because of this, Mapai was regularly attacked by Rhodesian and South African forces, and until recently minefields still surrounded the town. From Mapai there is a good, but very boring, gravel road to the south.

Mapai to Matsambo

At Chicumbane the road goes through the gate to enter the Limpopo National Park. Almost immediately the main track takes off westwards over the sandveld to the Shingwedzi drainage, but the more interesting track follows the western bank of the river all the way down to the Olifants confluence.

During the first part of the journey southwards, villages and their associated cleared fields are widely scattered along the river, and there are long stretches of mopane and mixed bush. Most of the villages and houses are set back from the river on the higher ground – the only indication of the floods that come every few years. The floods are essential to their system of farming, because they replenish the soil in the lands, but unfortunately the lands are usually cleared right up to the river, increasing the erosion risk, and the ecologically important gallery forest is usually cleared as well.

The road is rough – one seldom gets out of second gear – the surface is alluvial gravel and fine floodplain soil that sends up clouds of dust, and the bushes grow close into the sides of the track. Often the track disappears completely in the villages, and you have to work your way along myriad sled tracks, sometimes assisted by a friendly wave from the locals.

Along this stretch of the river you feel that you are very much in touch with it, even though the road is along the edge of the floodplain and there are usually ploughed lands between the road and the river. Every now and again wide vistas of the river open up, and there are regular cattle and sled tracks leading down to the river banks, giving an opportunity to pop down to the river and see it in different 'moods'.

Although this whole area is a national park, we saw very few game animals – just a pair of klipspringers and a duiker on this whole stretch. At one stream crossing we saw the spoor of a small group of elephants. This set us wondering how the impoverished local people would cope when more substantial numbers of elephants moved out of the Kruger National Park with the dropped fences, being thirsty for Limpopo water. The succulent crops along the river are bound to be a temptation.

Local transport is interesting in this area. The inhabitants are cut off from the outside world and seldom see vehicles. Much transport of goods is still done using the centuries-old method of ox sled that slips across the sand, with the occasional high two-wheeled ox cart with steel wheels. Some of the youngsters ride their oxen, and quite a few donkeys were in evidence, with the odd bicycle being the most cherished possession in wealthier families.

In the middle of nowhere we suddenly come across a homemade corrugated-iron boat chained to a tree, to help the locals get across the river when it is in flood. It is interesting that, in this area south of the Nuanedzi confluence, Ramke noted that 'here the native river craft were fashioned from tree bark and most primitive, further south dugouts were the rule'. The technology of forming corrugated iron around a frame may not be as different from the process of building a bark boat as it may at first seem.

Matsambo

Opposite the town of Combomune on the east bank there is a small administrative post at Matsambo, its white-painted walls jarring in the landscape after kilometres of mud-coloured villages. This is where the ancient trade route from Inhambane to the Soutpansberg crossed the Limpopo, which has been used for centuries by traders, hunters, missionaries and labour recruiters, as they linked the ports of Inhambane, Xai-Xai and Delagoa Bay with the inland kingdoms of Mapungubwe, Zimbabwe and Khami, and later the agricultural and mining economy of the European settlers. It is also the route followed by Roman Catholic priest Father Joaquim de Santa Rita Montanha and his party on a trade mission to the Boers at Schoemansdal in 1855.

Nearby is the site of Soshangane's (alias Manukosi's) kraal, and 10 kilometres to the south the track crosses the Djindi Stream at the site where the Van Rensburg Trek met their end at the hands of Soshangane's impis (see box on page 194).

Soon after Matsambo the low hills fade out, the countryside becomes very flat, and there is a rapid improvement in the alluvial soils. With better agricultural opportunities the density of villages increases, and this places some question marks against the future status of this area within a major national park.

OPPOSITE TOP: The exit and entrance gate to the Limpopo National Park at Chiveguemba downstream from the river crossing at Mapai.

OPPOSITE BOTTOM: Somewhere below Mapai following the west bank of the river, Peter's sons haul out a soccer ball in a remote village. There are many of these, and invariably it does not take long for the local kids to join in.

Like most Voortrekker leaders, Johannes Hendrik Janse van Rensburg (nicknamed Lang Hans) believed in God and the superiority of the white man, particularly the white Afrikaner. Tall and determined, and with a fierce temper, he and his party had fled the stifling rule of the British in the Eastern Cape, and headed north to find a place where they could live life according to their own rules.

After spending a short time with Louis Trichardt at Salt Pan, on the western end of the Soutpansberg, in early 1836 Lang Hans and his party headed for the coast at Delagoa Bay, or Inhambane, on a rather urgent quest to trade the large store of ivory they had accumulated by hunting and trading for powder, lead and other essential supplies. Ammunition had already been a problem on the way north, when they had split off from Louis Trichardt's party because of an argument over the responsible use of ammunition.

Lang Hans's party consisted of 10 Voortrekker men, 9 wives and 30 children, together with a number of coloured servants. They travelled with nine ox-wagons and a large number of stock, which together with the shortage of ammunition was to prove their undoing. According to one source, they had as many as 500 cattle, several thousand sheep and a substantial number of horses.

They stopped over for a week or two at the well-known business centre of Mashaokop (near the present-day missionary settlement at Elim) to find out about possible routes to Delagoa Bay, then headed down into the Lowveld along the centuries-old trading route to the coast.

The trek moved steadily eastwards at the leisurely pace of just eight kilometres a day, centred around the lumbering, heavily laden ox wagons, allowing time for the numerous stock to feed, and the men to hunt for the pot or reconnoitre the route ahead on horseback. After crossing the drift in the Shingwedzi River, around the end of July 1836 Lang Hans and his party approached the Limpopo River near 'Chief Sakana's' Village.

According to Shangaans interviewed later, they turned south towards the smaller Djindi River, to avoid the chief's village, along the route to one of the two main drifts across the Limpopo. Van Rensburg went ahead to recce the drift across the Limpopo, and shot a few hippos, which he gave to the chief. In spite of a warning that they should go no further because a 'Zulu impi' was approaching, Van Rensburg reportedly said that 'he would not be held up by any Zulu impi' and proceeded with his party to the Djindi River. There the steep-sided drift slowed them down, and by nightfall they had only managed to get five of the nine wagons to the other side. Instead of forming the well-known Voortrekker 'laager' (a rough circle of wagons), they camped just where they were, with the wagons in a long line, four to the north and five to the south of the small river, with the ends of the camp marked by stately baobab trees, and a large mahogany nearby, all of which still preside over the site.

It appears that Lang Hans underestimated the chief called Sakana who, after exhaustive historical research, has been identified as none other than the powerful and ruthless Soshangane, founder of the Gaza Kingdom and the Shangaan nation! Tsetse flies and droughts had made it difficult for Soshangane to accumulate cattle in the area, and the large herd of cattle and sheep accompanying the Voortrekkers would have attracted avaricious interest from the ruler. Another source[2] suggests that Soshangane feared that this trek was the first wave of a Boer attempt to take over his lands, so he acted quickly to resist this invasion.

Late that night the wagons suddenly found themselves under attack by Soshangane's impi, coming from a southerly direction. The first wagons were quickly overrun but, in spite of the surprise and the pitch darkness, the Trekkers put up tough resistance, and withdrew to the rear wagons. The attackers penetrated the line of ox wagons, and divided the Trekkers into four groups. Three were overpowered, but the fourth put up such a fight that the attackers were repeatedly repulsed. Thirty-five years later Erskine reported, 'The natives show a baobab-tree, where one of the two brave Boer leaders fell, fighting, side by side with their backs to the tree, with their men, and repulsing attack after attack'.

By daybreak their ammunition supplies were exhausted, and the warnings of Louis Trichardt were tragically realised. All of the party, including the coloured servants, were murdered, apart from the two Van Wyk children of six and four years old, who were protected and rescued under the shield of a warrior. These poor wretches were heard crying in a kraal by Jan Pretorius several months later, but died shortly thereafter from fever.

The tragedy was investigated repeatedly, first by Louis Trichardt, then Jan Pretorius and party, who had relatives in the Van Rensburg Trek, then two years later by Louis Trichardt's son Karel. All these visitors were not molested, but they may have come closer than they realised to sharing the same fate as Lang Hans van Rensburg. Over the following century the various pieces of the puzzle were gradually put together, and finally comprehensively clarified by a National Parks Board expedition to the site in 1959.

Apart from taking the animals and guns, Soshangane prohibited his people from removing things from the wagons, and later they were burned with all their contents. Two years later Karel Trichardt was able to bury the remaining bones of his countrymen. Bits of valuable iron were gradually removed from the charred remains, and 120 years later the Parks Board expedition was given an anvil that was clearly identifiable as belonging to the Van Rensburg Trek.

Louis Trichardt used the tragedy to motivate punishment of Soshangane and the Gaza Kingdom, which culminated in the arrest and banishment of Ngungunyane 29 years later.

A memorial garden to the Louis Trichardt and Van Rensburg Treks was erected in central Maputo in the 1960s, complete with carvings of ox wagons, granite stones proclaiming the greatness of these Afrikaner heroes, and a pond with a mosaic of the routes of the treks. In spite of the civil war in Mozambique, and no love lost between that country and the apartheid government, the memorial garden was not vandalised and is still well kept, as a somewhat bizarre reminder of the old days of southern Africa.

Olifants River

Twenty kilometres further on, our road turns off to the west at Mantavane, and follows through the mopane scrub to Massingir and the Massingir Dam, the largest dam in the whole Limpopo River System. This is the best place to cross the Olifants River, although there is apparently a drift that is sometimes passable down near the Olifants–Limpopo confluence. According to the early explorers, such as St Vincent Erskine, at the confluence there was an open lake more than two kilometres long and one kilometre wide.

The Olifants is by far the largest tributary of the Limpopo. It makes up about a quarter of the catchment area and a quarter of the total flow of the Limpopo River. It drains the higher rainfall part of the catchment in the Eastern Highlands, all the way from Pretoria. It flows through the platinum mining area of Sekhukhuneland, and then follows a long and pristine gorge through the Drakensberg that is popular for white-water rafting. After emerging into the Lowveld, its banks are lined with the various conservancies of the Valley of the Olifants, before it enters Kruger National Park and flows on to Massingir Dam. The dam wall has since been raised, which will unfortunately flood back into the Olifants Gorge on the Kruger National Park boundary.

Macarretane and Chokwe

From Massingir the route follows the tarred road to Macarretane and the Barrage. This derelict town was once a thriving centre, with many major buildings and a Portuguese-style hotel. However, it was completely submerged during the 2000 floods, as shown by the high-water marks still visible on some buildings. The Barrage is really a large weir that supplies water through a system of canals to a huge agricultural irrigation scheme in the Chokwe area, which provides much of the food for Maputo and the southern part of Mozambique. The Massingir Dam is an integral part of this system, since it is built to release water during the dry season to allow year-round irrigation. This water supply is complemented by regular flooding of the broad floodplain, which replenishes the soil every few years.

OPPOSITE TOP: With the opening of the Limpopo National Park in Mozambique, and the removal of the boundary fence, elephants from the burgeoning Kruger herds did not take long to occupy the area.

OPPOSITE BOTTOM: Graceful fever-trees occupy a grazed area utilised by the frequently seen Nguni cattle which constitute the main wealth of people living in these remote areas.

The Barrage also acts as an important bridge across the Limpopo – the first crossing structure over the river in the 450 kilometres from Beit Bridge. It was substantially damaged during the floods, but has recently been repaired and upgraded, as has the Macarretane railway station, and the line is back in action. It is therefore a key crossroads' area, with one leg going up to Massingir, another down to Chokwe and Macia, and then up to Chicualacuala and down to Guija and Chibuto on the eastern side. A major informal trading centre has already developed on the higher ground east of the Barrage.

The Barrage pushes back a few kilometres, and even provided habitat for a lonely hippo during one of our visits. A slow drive up along the river covers seemingly endless agricultural lands, and the shells of Portuguese-style farmhouses show that the commercial lands stretched well above the Barrage in colonial days.

Right next to the Barrage, Xirrundzo Hill provides a commanding view, and this high ground presented an important refuge during the 2000 floods, with the Roman Catholic Seminary playing a key role in humanitarian efforts.

Twenty kilometres below the Barrage the bridge that provided a link between the agricultural centre of Chokwe and the administrative centre of Guija was completely washed away in the floods. This means that, while Chokwe forged ahead with aid-funded agricultural development, Guija lagged behind – until recently when a new tarred road linking Guija southwards to Chibuto was opened.

Of the two roads to the south, the eastern leg from Guija to Chibuto is much more interesting. The road is mostly raised above the wide floodplain and touches the river in several places as it meanders gently through the agricultural lands. By now all the silt has been deposited from the slow-moving water, and the river is crystal clear, with numerous water plants. At Chaimite the site where Ngungunyane was captured is marked with a monument and outdoor museum (see box on page 200).

Chibuto

After many kilometres across the flats, the road suddenly climbs about 100 metres up on top of the ridge at Chibuto, the administrative capital of the district, and the rapidly growing centre of a new heavy sand dune mining development. It is just below Chibuto that the other major drainage in Mozambique, the Changane River, joins the Limpopo. Although it drains a large area, up to quite close to the Sabi River, the rainfall is generally low, and the river flow is very seasonal. *The Limpopo River Basin Atlas* describes its marshy nature as follows: 'Even in the months following the rains, much of the river is better described as a swamp.' Nevertheless, it is interesting because it includes the Banhine National Park which contains an unusual wetland

Ngungunyane's capture at Chaimite

The Portuguese cavalry of Mouzinho de Albuquerque galloped up and surrounded the dignified, heavily built, middle-aged man sitting under the marula tree at Chaimite.

The man was Ngungunyane, the 'Lion of Gaza' and the last king of the Gaza Kingdom, which had ruled the inland areas of most of southern Mozambique for 60 years. It had been started by his grandfather, Soshangane, an Ndwandwe chief who escaped the wrath of Shaka, king of the Zulus, in the early 1830s. The Gaza Kingdom outlasted not only the power structures of the other Ndwandwe warlords who played a significant role in Mozambique, such as Nxaba, Metangula, Maseko and Gwangwara, but the Zulu monarchy itself.

Soshangane, who mostly called himself Manukosi in Mozambique, had conquered most of the Tsonga chieftaincies south of the Sabi River, absorbed the young men into his armies, taken over the women as wives for his leaders,

demanded tribute from the local populations, and carried out raids into what is now the South African Lowveld and Zimbabwe to increase his cattle herds. He established his son, Umzila, in the uplands to the north, between the Sabi and Zambezi rivers, and moved his own capital around, first from Bilene to the Combomune area, then back to Chaimite. On his death there had been a debilitating power struggle for six years between two of his sons, Mawewe and Umzila, which was eventually won by the latter.

After Umzila's death, Ngungunyane, who was not the legitimate heir to the throne, moved swiftly to seize power and consolidate it, ahead of his elder brother. With the rapidly increasing interest of the colonial powers, particularly the British, Dutch and Portuguese, he had reduced, rather than expanded, the area under his control, uprooting his capital and more than 50 000 of his people on the Zimbabwean plateau, and moving down to Manjacaze. He played the powers off ecosystem with a large area alternating between swamp and dry plain on a roughly seven-year cycle. This park is an important waterbird habitat, and has a number of species occurring way out of their normal range.

From Chibuto one road dips down onto the floodplain and crosses the river at the only bridge that stayed open during the 2000 floods. This whole floodplain was covered for many kilometres, and it is near here that the world's imagination was captured by television images of mother and baby Rositha Pedro being winched out of the tree where she was born.

Another road heads off east to Manjacaze, which was a later capital of Ngungunyane's, and has a monument to his memory. The other road heads down to the main coastal road, the EN1 highway close to Xai-Xai.

against one another, generally favouring the Portuguese. But as he consolidated southwards he came more and more into conflict with the local Chopi, who had the backing of the Portuguese.

Skirmishes with the local chiefs were not always won by Ngungunyane, and his power was gradually eroded. In an increasingly difficult situation, with the Portuguese becoming more demanding, Ngungunyane tried his best to negotiate and avoid a head-on confrontation with the Portuguese, against the belligerent urgings of some of his advisers, particularly Maguiguana, who later led a final Shangaan rebellion against the Portuguese. Eventually the bold and ambitious new Portuguese Royal Commissioner, António Enes, built up a substantial force of 2 000 European soldiers with machine guns and repeating rifles, which defeated Ngungunyane's impis at the decisive Battle of Coolela, close to Manjacaze. It was shortly after this that Ngungunyane moved with a small group

to Chaimite, where his grandfather Soshangane lay buried, and resigned himself to his fate.

As with so much of history, our perceptions of Ngungunyane's character depends on whose accounts we are reading, or who we are talking to. A Swedish missionary who lived close to him for several years focused on his drinking and his many women; to some Portuguese he was a troublemaker and dangerous enemy; and to some of his subjects who had been conquered, such as the Chopi, he was a tyrant. However, several European writers were dazzled by his power, and the British South Africa Company considered him 'far more powerful a chief than Lobengula'. Despite his ultimate downfall, in the face of unstoppable technology, the 'Lion of Gaza' probably deserves the place he fills as the most important African monarch in recent Mozambican history. To the present-day occupants of southern Mozambique, he is a great hero of the struggle against colonialism.[3]

Xai-Xai

The evocative name 'Xai-Xai' is said to have come from the noise of the wind through the reeds, which is a clear association with the river. However, apart from the main bridge over the Limpopo at its western entrance, Xai-Xai is a town that seems to have 'turned its back' on the river. We could find no sites that actively made use of views of the river. In the main gathering place, the plaza, views of the river are blocked off by a wall and embankment to protect the town from floods. These did not help much in 2000, when rescue boats were motoring up to first-floor windows to rescue inhabitants! It is significant that the more up-market part of the town is on the ridge to the south, out of the way of floods.

Xai-Xai is the capital of Gaza Province, and was the main port in the Limpopo River, even though it is about 50 kilometres upstream from the river mouth. Early in the twentieth century tiny coastal steamers carrying labourers recruited by WNLA used to leave from the small wharf, bound for Maputo and the train to the Witwatersrand. Its proximity to the sea can be seen in the river itself, which is tidal – so that the river flows both ways, depending on whether the tide is flowing in or out. The water did not look very suitable for human consumption, and is sure to be salty.

At Xai-Xai the Limpopo River floodplain is about eight kilometres wide, and is clearly made up of good soils, with lots of favourable grazing for the large numbers of Nguni cattle, and extensive vegetable farms. Where not cultivated it is mostly grassland, with occasional patches of trees or bush. A really interesting route is to head through the market out to the floodplain and away from the town, following the river towards the mouth. It gives a good perspective on the extent of the floodplain, and how the river meanders slowly through it, taking more than 50 kilometres by river to cover a straight-line distance of 23 kilometres.

The River Mouth

On the eastern side of the river, the floodplain track works its way down to the edge of the coastal dunes, where most of the villages are perched on higher ground. The dark black soil planted with rice and vegetables shows how productive these floodplains are, and also gives a clue as to how inaccessible they are to vehicles during the wet season.

Shortly before the mouth on the eastern side there is a coconut plantation, followed by the coastal fore-dune and the mouth itself. Around the mouth are extensive mangrove forests.

On the western side, the road to the mouth travels on higher ground for some distance, but then drops down close to the river, where locals can be seen fishing and netting prawns. The 'Port Captain' used to control the ships and boats moving in and out of the mouth, and there is still an anchorage for smaller pleasure craft. An old lighthouse on the hill used to guide mariners coming into the anchorage. At the mouth itself is Zongoene Lodge, which provides a blend of experiences up the river, on the dunes, on the beach and out to sea.

The Limpopo National Park, the Great Limpopo Transfrontier Park and the Broader Transfrontier Conservation Area

The triangular area between the Limpopo, the Olifants and the Kruger Park boundary used to be a well-known elephant hunting zone. A century ago it was one of the main hunting grounds of illegal ivory hunters such as Bvekenya Barnard (see box on page 174). After that it was a formally proclaimed hunting area known as 'Coutada 16', where the tradition of nefarious activities was carried on. In the early 1990s there were accusations of professional hunters breaking holes in the border fence and baiting lions to come through from Kruger National Park, so that rich clients could shoot them.

As early as 1938, the linking of the Kruger National Park, Coutada 16 and Gonarezhou National Park in Zimbabwe was mooted, and this type of thinking gathered momentum with initiatives leading to the establishment of the Peace Parks Foundation in the mid-1990s. After the Mozambique Peace Accord of 1992, feasibility studies were carried out and, in 2000, a formal agreement to link the three areas, as well as others, was made between the governments of Mozambique, South Africa and Zimbabwe.

One of the first steps taken by the Mozambican Government to implement the formal agreement was to change the legal status of Coutada 16 to that of Limpopo National Park, and a formal treaty establishing the Great Limpopo Transfrontier

Park was signed by the Heads of State right next to the Limpopo River in Xai-Xai in December 2002.

The most impressive aspect of the project is its size. As a start, Kruger National Park, Makuleke and its western contractual areas make up about 2.5 million hectares. Then the Limpopo National Park adds another million, giving 3.5 million hectares, or 35 000 square kilometres, for the whole Transfrontier Park. If plans are realised to include Gonarezhou National Park, Zinave National Park and Banhine National Park, as well as a host of communal areas in between, the total Transfrontier Conservation Area will be nearly 10 million hectares, or 100 000 square kilometres, making it one of the largest conservation areas in the world.

The implementation of such a visionary concept will not be easy, and there are a number of serious questions that remain. The Peace Parks Foundation, working with all parties concerned, is determined to see the concept succeed in spite of massive rhino poaching emanating from the Mozambique side since 2008. Obviously the internationally famous and well-established Kruger National Park forms a core on which to build, but new approaches to accommodating people within parks provide many management challenges not least the protection of the wildlife resource.

The objectives of the Limpopo National Park say that communities must participate in decision-making and benefit from economic opportunities and resources produced by the Park. It has also been made quite clear that nobody in the Park may be translocated against their will. After careful negotiations, and substantial investment in alternative areas, the 6 000-odd community members living in the Shingwedzi River Valley have agreed to move, but it may take years to finalise. Without this key wildlife tourism zone, it is questionable whether the Park is really viable, because so many tourists have expectations of a wild bush experience. Unfortunately the best areas for game viewing are the riverine habitats that are also preferred for agriculture.

If these and other problems can be overcome, the Great Limpopo Transfrontier Park and its accompanying Transfrontier Conservation Area will be a model for the future, showing how governments of different countries, conservationists, tourism operators and local communities can work together to create bold new sustainable land-use initiatives based on extended conservation areas that form the core of major tourism destinations.

OPPOSITE TOP: The town of Chokwe east of Massingir Dam is a bustling centre providing the needs of a vast number of people, many of whom are engaged in the activity of flood-plain agriculture centred around a huge irrigation scheme supplying much of the food for the capital of Maputo.

OPPOSITE BOTTOM: The government installed irrigation canals to divert the abundant waters of the Limpopo and Olifants rivers stored in the Massingir Dam and used in the floodplain agriculture.

Early Trade Routes, Explorers, Traders, Surveyors and Missionaries

The Limpopo Valley has had traders moving through it for well over a thousand years. As happened elsewhere in Africa and Asia, the ancient trade routes seem to have followed tracks originally made by migrating elephant and game. Routes favoured gorges through mountain ranges and followed reliable water sources, or at least linked between known permanent waterholes. Water sources were very important because water was not carried by the porters as it would lower their capacity to carry goods. Various Shangaan-Tsonga, Sotho and Venda groups used these initial tracks for their extensive trade activities with the east coast.[4]

One of the ancient trade routes went all the way down the Limpopo, at least until about Chaimite, but the main ones moved in a generally east–west direction across the Limpopo River, from Inhambane or Bazaruto Islands to Mapungubwe or the settlements south of the Soutpansberg. There were two main crossing points, one up near Pafuri, and one further down at Matsambo near Combomune. Unfortunately very little was recorded of the routes used by black and Arab traders, and we have to rely on the written record of the later Europeans to find out what the tracks across the Limpopo were like in the early days. One of the earliest written record of these trade routes was provided by Father Joaquim Montanha, a Roman Catholic priest who led a trade mission from Inhambane to the Boer settlers in the Soutpansberg in 1855. Part of his instructions was to keep a detailed diary, and this contains interesting descriptions of the landscape and the people along the route.[5] Unfortunately he did not write much about the Limpopo River, apart from saying that they stopped on the eastern side and had to keep quiet because Manukosi's (Soshangane's) kraal was just two days away, and they were not sure how friendly he would be. Luckily he was not there, and there were no problems.

The first person to leave a written record of travelling *along* the Limpopo in Mozambique was Louis Trichardt, who visited Matsambo on a rapid horse patrol to investigate the fate of the Van Rensburg Trek. When leaving the site, somewhat in fear of their own lives, they travelled northwards all along the river to the Pafuri area, where they turned westwards on the trade routes back to Salt Pan. In 1868 St Vincent Erskine set out to 'discover' the mouth of the Limpopo, and left many useful descriptions of his trip, as well as later trips to visit Umzila, during which he made detours along the river (see box on page 208).

OPPOSITE TOP: The main bridge spanning the, by now, wide and full Limpopo River at the entrance to the town of Xai-Xai serves the needs of the north–south main route traffic from Maputo.

OPPOSITE BOTTOM: The beautiful Portuguese-built administrative centre in the town of Xai-Xai, formerly João Belo. The departing Portuguese left little, apart from their architecture, often beautiful and sadly abandoned, reminding us of their long-held presence in this land.

It seems difficult to imagine that, after the Mozambique coast had been inhabited for centuries by black Africans, Arabs and Portuguese, the English-speaking world did not know where the mouth of the Limpopo River was. Up to 1850 Cornwallis Harris and Adulphe Delegorgue, the explorers and hunters, believed that it ended in Delagoa Bay. Thomas Baines discounted that, but was not sure where it actually ended. Then a hunter called Gassiott recorded that the Boers he had encountered believed that it ended at Inhambane.[6] This was the background to Erskine's trip to 'discover' the mouth of the Limpopo in 1868.[7]

Erskine was a young civil servant who came from an aristocratic background, and his father was the Natal Colonial Secretary. The accounts of his later expeditions show that he was clearly an imperialist, who had visions of encircling the Boers with British territory, and he was quite explicit about how much he despised the Portuguese. Nevertheless, his first expedition, at the age of 22, appears to have been motivated by a youthful lust for adventure, and the hope that he could make a name for himself.

He had originally planned to join the German explorer Karl Mauch on an expedition to Mzilikazi, but in Lydenburg he decided to go his own way and solve the riddle of the river mouth. He walked down along the Olifants River with one servant from Natal, and a small number of porters, staying over at local kraals along the way. He purchased food and porter services with a stock of beads, cloth and brass wire.

He was also trained in surveying, and took sextant readings at most important places, to aid with mapping the area later. On reaching the confluence with the Limpopo after a month, he remarked on the large lake, and the 'immense flocks of green parrots which perched in the trees … awaiting an opportunity to swoop down into the corn'. Sadly these parrots are now scarce along the river.

Unfortunately he found that his servant had

helped himself to a large portion of the beads which were to be used to buy food and services. This cost him dearly later when he could hardly pay his way, and the local chiefs and their subjects harassed him continuously, until he got a measure of help from some traders he knew.

Erskine was pretty much at the mercy of the local chiefs, especially Umzila's headman, Manjobo. In spite of the harassment, poor food, bouts of fever, and often having to carry his own heavy loads, he made it to the mouth of the river on his own, 10 weeks after leaving Lydenburg, recording his observations and taking sextant readings along the way. After all this, it seems he was actually a bit disappointed in the mouth itself!

In spite of the difficulties encountered, the resourceful Erskine looked for more adventure, and in 1871 was asked by the Lieutenant Governor of Natal to visit Umzila in the Manica highlands.[8] After landing at Inhambane he trekked back to the lower Limpopo, and used a wood-and-canvas double canoe with a sail to go down the river to the mouth from 'Manjobo's Kraal' at about Chaimite. He was investigating the navigability of this stretch of the river for larger vessels and reported as follows: 'The navigable and commercial capabilities of the Limpopo may be summed up thus: It is difficult of entry, and has 60 miles [96 km] of navigable water, reaching 25 miles [40 km] in a direct line, and flowing through a fine alluvial valley 15 miles [24 km] broad. The productions are hides, horns, native furs, gums, ground-nuts, vegetable ivory, ivory, orchilla lichen, mangrove poles, perhaps a little cotton (which grows wild here and is used by the natives), honey and beeswax …'

Erskine carried out several more exploration, political and trade trips in Mozambique and elsewhere in southern Africa. He also went to the Transvaal as a government surveyor, and ended up as a mining engineer on the Witwatersrand. His detailed observations recorded in his reports and journal give a useful record of the Limpopo as it was in the late 1800s.

The Agricultural Schemes

The lower part of the Limpopo Basin in Mozambique is quite different from the upper parts, because there is a wide floodplain of rich alluvial soils with high production potential. These good soils start quite suddenly at Malaamba, 30 kilometres north of the Olifants confluence, and at the Shingwedzi confluence on the Olifants River, and stretch all the way to the coast.[9] Where there is irrigation many families are able to plant two and even three crops a year. This is also the area most affected by floods, so families have to trade off the rich soils with the risk of losing most of their crop every few years.

In order to make effective use of these soils, the government built a major irrigation scheme in the Chokwe area, called the Limpopo Valley Scheme. It is the largest irrigation scheme in the country, with more than 25 000 hectares under irrigation. The politics and 'social engineering' approach followed by this scheme has changed several times with the political changes in the country and, in a way, is a microcosm of the broader situation in Mozambique.

The agricultural potential was recognised in the early 1900s, and several proposals for major irrigation schemes were made. But not much was done until 1950 when the head of a government survey team, Trigo de Morais, was put in charge of implementing the proposal he had made 25 years earlier. This was for a barrage at Macarretane, with a road and railway bridge over it to link to Zimbabwe. The barrage acts as a weir, diverting water at a constant level into a massive system of 200 kilometres of canals and 1 450 kilometres of irrigation flumes. The whole irrigation system is managed and maintained by a state service enterprise now called SIREMO, the Eduardo Mondlane Irrigation System.

In order to establish the farms, about 2 000 existing peasant farmer families were removed from the land, and white Portuguese peasants settled there, with substantial subsidies of transport, infrastructure and equipment as incentives to encourage commercial production. This reflected the philosophy of Salazar, Prime Minister of Portugal, to encourage peasants to move from Portugal to the 'overseas provinces'.

Later, when Portugal was trying to show that it was different from other colonial powers, substantial numbers of black *assimilados* (who had some education and adopted Portuguese language and customs) were also allowed to join these *colonatos*.[10] Although extremely costly, by this time the Limpopo Valley Scheme was producing about half of the national rice output, as well as wheat, vegetables and fruit.

At independence, thousands of Mozambican peasants entered the *colonato* and replaced the departing Portuguese settlers. When farmers were evacuated when the Limpopo flooded its banks in 1977, the government seized the opportunity and prevented the farmers from returning to their land. Instead it was incorporated in huge state farms, following the socialist centrally planned model, with price fixing and major state funding. Having been kicked off their land for a second time, it is not surprising that the locals were uncooperative, and refused to provide labour, which became a major problem during peak periods, largely brought on by the focus on a single crop, rice.

By 1981 it was acknowledged that the state farms were not working, and with Frelimo's move away from Marxism at the Fourth Congress, a new direction of more decentralised, market-orientated, small-scale farming projects was established. In particular, both government aid and interference in market forces were substantially reduced.

International aid organisations tried to fill the gap, but only with limited success. Over the last three decades, and particularly since the end of the civil war, the system has become more settled. Many families have plots on the irrigated floodplain, as well as on the non-irrigated sandy hills, which allows them to escape the floods more easily, and to produce a diversity of crops. Maize is now the preferred staple food throughout the Limpopo Basin, and rice has been drastically reduced. In the densely populated district of Xai-Xai, land scarcity and easy access to the Maputo market has influenced farmers to grow higher value crops, such as vegetables.

BELOW: Early morning finds women on their way to market in Xai-Xai, walking parallel to an irrigation channel and the Limpopo River. The land below the town is highly fertile and supplies all their daily needs.

Floods

For the people of the Lower Limpopo Valley, floods are a major part of their lives. Not only have almost all families been touched by a recent flood in some way or other, but the 'threat of the next flood' looms large in the psyche of the valley. At the same time their livelihood depends on the floods, because they play an essential role in regenerating the soil and flushing out stagnant wetlands.

The Limpopo Basin has suffered a number of severe floods in the last 50 years, particularly in 1955, 1967, 1972, 1975, 1977, 1981 and 2000. The floods of 2000 were by far the worst, with water levels at heights not seen since 1948.

The peak floods are obviously the most dramatic, but water-level statistics from Chokwe show that mild or moderate floods occur in half of all years. Mild floods (with river levels of 4–6 metres) occurred seven times in a 32-year period from 1953–94, and moderate floods (6–8 metres) nine times during this period. Severe floods are those over 8 metres, and the 2000 floods hit 10.5 metres. At least that is what they estimate, because the measuring equipment was all under water! An extra metre or two may not sound much but, given the width of the very gently sloping floodplain, it can make a huge difference to the area that is flooded.

Flooding in Mozambique is caused by a number of factors, including heavy localised rainfall, tropical cyclone activity and the poor management of upstream dams and wetlands in other parts of southern Africa. The floods of 2000 have been blamed on record rainfall, three tropical cyclones on top of one another, and mismanagement of dams, wetlands and river courses, sometimes far away in the catchment areas. The clogging of rivers right up the Crocodile to near Hartbeespoort Dam was acknowledged to have caused a build-up of water that contributed to the peak when it all flushed out in a rush.

Flooding, as well as disaster measures needed to cope with floods, have placed an enormous financial burden on Mozambique, which is already one of the world's poorest countries. The 2000 floods are estimated to have cost the equivalent of 20 per cent of Mozambique's gross domestic product (GDP).

Of course, the loss of human life, and the human suffering caused, especially when flood waters rise suddenly, are the highest cost. Very few people who witnessed the dramatic scenes broadcast around the world in 2000 would not have been touched by the human tragedy during the peak flood. However, the most difficult part comes afterwards. For those who survive the initial flooding, there is a high likelihood of broken or fractured bones from swift-moving, debris-filled waters, and floods bring the threat of water-borne diseases, such as cholera, dysentery and diarrhoea. In addition, quiet receding waters create ideal breeding grounds for malaria mosquitoes.

There are also major losses of crops and livestock. Although the lands are improved by the deposited soil, the present year's crops are often ruined, just at the time when the families most need them, although this depends on the timing of the floods in relation to planting and harvest.

During the 2000 floods more than 13 000 cattle were lost along the Limpopo's main branch. In Chicualacuala, the sudden force of the flood wave was sufficient to sweep cattle into the current, while downstream thousands were lost when pastures turned into lakes.

The cities and towns and infrastructure are also dramatically affected. Bridges and electricity lines are washed away, and buildings damaged. In Xai-Xai city 65 000 people, living in about 13 000 traditional homes, made of cane, bamboo, palm, grass-thatching and other vegetation, lost their homes in the flood.

The humanitarian efforts need to last for some while after the floods, but the benefits soon start to appear. One of the unexpected benefits of the 2000 floods has been an increase in the amount and types of fish available in the river around Chokwe. And after the ground dries out, the replenished soil usually leads to bumper crops for the next few years, if families can assemble the equipment, seed and labour needed to plant at the right time.

Floods are very much part of the 'circle of life' of this great river and, despite the drama and human tragedy when really high floods occur, the livelihoods of the people are well tuned into the ecology of the Limpopo System.

Coastal Trade[11]

The history of the Limpopo River Mouth needs to be seen in the context of the development (or lack of development) of the coastal area of southern Mozambique.

Before the Portuguese arrived in the area around 1500, most of the Mozambique coast was inhabited by people whom they called 'Tonga' (as opposed to the 'Tsonga' who invaded from the south later), living in small groups and eating fish and shellfish from the coast, with some crops, but not farmed on a large scale. It appears that these people had very few cattle, mostly due to the presence of tsetse fly.

There were no large towns in the area, and the major trading settlements of the Indian Ocean trade did not stretch as far south as this. The most southerly trading centre was at Sofala at Beira. Later the Arabs may have traded as far south as Inhambane, but Cape Corrientes just south of this was the traditional southern limit of navigation in the Indian Ocean prescribed by the Arab navigators, because south of this the weather deteriorated, the trade winds became less reliable and the strong currents become more dangerous. In addition, it was just too far from the activities on the east coast of Africa. There is no evidence of Muslim commercial contact with the Limpopo or with Delagoa Bay itself. The gold, ivory and animal skins from the Mapungubwe area appear to have been carried overland directly to Sofala, and there was just not very much of sufficient value to justify carrying it all the way to the coast, apart from small quantities of copper and iron.

When the Portuguese set up their main trading, replenishment and ship-repair centre at Mozambique Island in the early sixteenth century, which served the East India route, the situation did not change immediately, until a ship's captain called Lourenço Marques explored the possibility of trade with the people of the southern river estuaries. By then the royal Portuguese 'factory' on Mozambique Island was working to establish an effective ivory trade, and every year sent ships to Inhambane, Delagoa Bay and the Limpopo Mouth.

A key component of the trade in the estuaries was that the larger sea-going ships were very vulnerable to the rapidly changing sand-bars, and seldom ventured far into the estuaries unless they were hiding from enemy ships. For this reason the traders would have been mostly confined to their larger ships, and would have been served by shallow draft vessels capable of going into estuaries without putting the major cargo supply on the 'mother ship' at risk.

OPPOSITE: Fish is an important source of protein in the diet of people living along the coast, and we found an abundance of fish available, including hawkers selling prawns which the area is famous for. This local woman had an excellent day's catch at Port Captain near the mouth of the river.

At this stage neither Inhambane, Delagoa Bay nor Limpopo Mouth was much of a settlement, but the wealth created by the trade (even if it was at a low level) allowed the local chiefs to spread their authority. The Portuguese traded almost exclusively with beads and cloth, both of which were luxury goods, and made little difference to the lives of the peasants of the area. There was also a demand for iron, since shipwrecked sailors were usually able to look after themselves by trading nails rescued from the wrecks.

While the main trade goods were ivory, the ships also bought food for their own use, but never on the scale needed to supply permanent garrisons and passing ships, as occurred further to the north. This low level of trade, focused primarily on ivory, continued for about a century, and the three estuaries became the points to which the people of the interior south of the Sabi came to trade with the outside world. However, after about 1660, the southern ivory could not compete with the more easily accessible and cheaper ivory from East Africa, and the cost of sending a regular trading ship southwards became too much, particularly in the light of pressure from the Dutch and English.

At the same time the more organised and warlike Tsongas were moving northwards from Delagoa Bay and dealing harshly with the local Tongas who were either absorbed or driven to the more marginal swamps and sand dunes, where they sometimes lived in houses built on stilts over the water to get away from their land-loving enemies.

In 1721 the Dutch tried to establish a permanent settlement at Delagoa Bay, but it only lasted for nine years, having been destroyed by English pirates during that period. It is likely that they visited the Limpopo Mouth, which was recognised as an anchorage, but trade levels remained low.

For most of the eighteenth century there was regular activity of pirates from different nations in this part of the Indian Ocean, particularly the French corsairs during the Revolutionary wars. It is likely that the Limpopo Mouth was visited irregularly by these privateers, but there appears to be no written record.

With increased economic activity in Delagoa Bay by Dutch and English ships, whaling also became an important activity in the area, based on the whales moving up and down the coast, but it is not known whether whaling ships used the Limpopo River Mouth to any great extent.

The invasions of the various Nguni groups in the early part of the nineteenth century virtually killed off the gold trade, and the main 'commodity' of trading along the coast quickly became slaves (see opposite).

Xai-Xai, known during the colonial period as João Belo, continued as a viable port. The coastal village nearby was known as Xai-Xai and a former favourite holiday resort, popular with South Africans. A 1931 report on shipping in Mozambique[12] listed it as one of a group of six secondary ports, behind the main ports of Lourenço Marques (Maputo) and Beira. It was probably only afterwards, with the building of dams in the catchment, that the general drying out of the river took place, and the blockage of the mouth by a sand-bar made shipping too dangerous.

Slavery[13]

We sometimes forget that slavery was part of the everyday way of life for most civilisations for thousands of years, and it is only in the last two centuries that the general public became sufficiently enlightened to put a stop to it. The transition from slavery-based labour to voluntary-paid labour coincided with the rapid expansion of European influence throughout the world, which nevertheless created demand for a slave trade of frightening proportions in the decades before it was finally abolished.

Along the Mozambique coast the carrying off of slaves was common practice in intertribal warfare, and slaves were widely used by the Arabs. Early historians record that in the 1760s the northward movement of the Tsonga chiefs and their conquest of the Lowveld between the Limpopo and Sabi generated a large supply of slaves at Inhambane. In spite of this, by the 1770s the annual slave trade for the whole of Mozambique was estimated at less than 2 000. This was soon to change.

The beginnings of the great Mozambique drought around 1820, with the subsequent banditry and social dislocation, played a major role in filling the baracoons with slaves. In fact, the coming of drought and locusts leading to disease, migration, warfare and slaving created a cycle of violence and social anarchy that has recurred many times in Mozambique's history.

With increasing restrictions on slaves coming out of West Africa, prices rose, and volumes of slaves exported from East Africa rose rapidly to fill the gap. It is estimated that between 1825 and 1830 around 20 000 slaves were exported out of Mozambique annually, mostly to the growing sugar plantations of the Indian Ocean islands, but some to as far away as Brazil and the United States. In the nineteenth century more than a million Africans were probably shipped out of Mozambican ports. The Limpopo didn't handle as many as the more northern ports, but the slave graveyard near the mouth shows that this river did not escape this human tragedy.

Although Britain persuaded Portugal to abolish the slave trade in 1836, this merely drove the slave trade 'underground', and increased demand. It was finally decided in 1858 to abolish slavery 20 years later. Meanwhile all sorts of euphemisms were developed to pay lip service to the freeing of slaves, but in the implementation little had changed. In 1878 a new labour law officially brought an end to all forms of slavery, but even then there were a few loopholes that were exploited by administrators in the field for decades. Soon after, the strong demand for labour on the rapidly expanding South African diamond and gold mines resulted in thousands of paid labourers being recruited in Mozambique, particularly in the Limpopo Valley.

For most of the traders along the Mozambique coast, slaves were just another commodity to be sold and transported as they pleased. It is difficult for us to imagine the horrors of this for the slaves, the disruption of their lives, families and complete and utter loss of dignity.

OPPOSITE: On the eastern side of the river a sandy track wends its way down to the coastal dunes and the mouth of the river, where the rich soils provide an abundance of trees and flowering plants to delight anyone.

FOLLOWING SPREAD: The site of the original Port Captain, who used to control vessels coming in and out of the river mouth, is now surrounded by a beautiful stretch of beach, palm trees and mangrove trees.

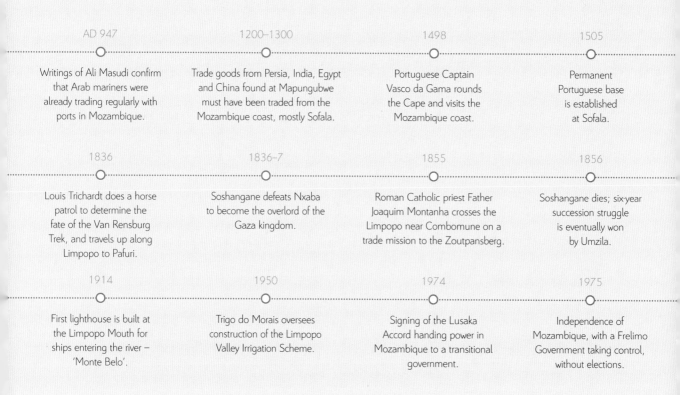

Mozambique section timeline

AD 947	1200–1300	1498	1505
Writings of Ali Masudi confirm that Arab mariners were already trading regularly with ports in Mozambique.	Trade goods from Persia, India, Egypt and China found at Mapungubwe must have been traded from the Mozambique coast, mostly Sofala.	Portuguese Captain Vasco da Gama rounds the Cape and visits the Mozambique coast.	Permanent Portuguese base is established at Sofala.

1836	1836–7	1855	1856
Louis Trichardt does a horse patrol to determine the fate of the Van Rensburg Trek, and travels up along Limpopo to Pafuri.	Soshangane defeats Nxaba to become the overlord of the Gaza kingdom.	Roman Catholic priest Father Joaquim Montanha crosses the Limpopo near Combomune on a trade mission to the Zoutpansberg.	Soshangane dies; six-year succession struggle is eventually won by Umzila.

1914	1950	1974	1975
First lighthouse is built at the Limpopo Mouth for ships entering the river – 'Monte Belo'.	Trigo do Morais oversees construction of the Limpopo Valley Irrigation Scheme.	Signing of the Lusaka Accord handing power in Mozambique to a transitional government.	Independence of Mozambique, with a Frelimo Government taking control, without elections.

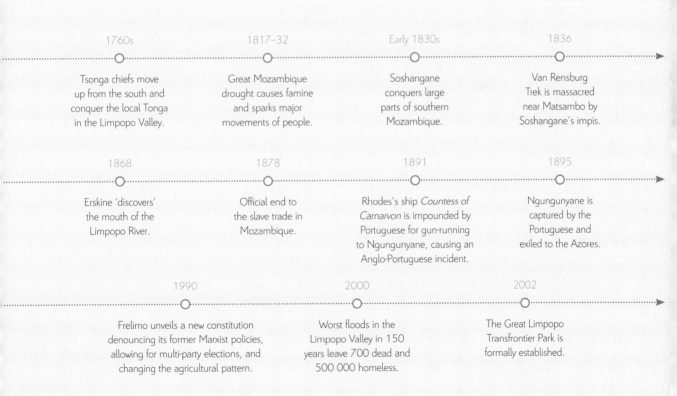

1760s	1817–32	Early 1830s	1836
Tsonga chiefs move up from the south and conquer the local Tonga in the Limpopo Valley.	Great Mozambique drought causes famine and sparks major movements of people.	Soshangane conquers large parts of southern Mozambique.	Van Rensburg Trek is massacred near Matsambo by Soshangane's impis.

1868	1878	1891	1895
Erskine 'discovers' the mouth of the Limpopo River.	Official end to the slave trade in Mozambique.	Rhodes's ship *Countess of Carnarvon* is impounded by Portuguese for gun-running to Ngungunyane, causing an Anglo-Portuguese incident.	Ngungunyane is captured by the Portuguese and exiled to the Azores.

1990	2000	2002
Frelimo unveils a new constitution denouncing its former Marxist policies, allowing for multi-party elections, and changing the agricultural pattern.	Worst floods in the Limpopo Valley in 150 years leave 700 dead and 500 000 homeless.	The Great Limpopo Transfrontier Park is formally established.

Afterword:
Dr John Ledger

'No man ever steps in the
same river twice, for it's not
the same river and he's not
the same man.'

– HERACLITUS C. 535–475 BC

Afterword

My first encounter with the Limpopo River was in 1960. My uncle had a farm in the Soutpansberg, which he only visited occasionally, being at that time the Dean of the Wits University Medical School. My father borrowed Uncle Eustace's rather smart black Citroën motor car, which had a strange gear lever sticking out of the dashboard, and the Ledgers went off to Molozi farm for a holiday and an adventure into the Kruger National Park. We set off on the road to Punda Maria in the dark and, driving into the rising sun on the dusty road, my father very nearly destroyed the entrance gate to the Park as he only saw it at the last moment and we arrived in a cloud of dust with all four wheels skidding on the gravel.

Visiting the Pafuri picnic site, I photographed my 14-year-old younger brother (Brian) and my parents (Jean and Jack) posing by a tree on the banks of the Limpopo.

We went on to Crooks' Corner, and were intrigued by the name, speculating about what kind of crooks might have roamed these riverine woodlands with ill intent. This fine book, *River of Gold*, will ensure that future visitors to Crooks' Corner have access to the information that we so lacked over half a century ago.

My own life has touched the Limpopo in a few fleeting ways, the first being that I was born, went to university, and have worked and lived in the City of Gold for most of my life. At the University of the Witwatersrand there is a spot in the courtyard of a famous pub called 'The Blind Pig', where one can see drops of rain moving south on the start of their journey to the Atlantic Ocean, while others nearby move north on their arduous trip to the Indian Ocean. Further east along the Witwatersrand Ridge, the south-flowing droplets do something unusual, by forming the headwaters of the Jukskei River, the most southerly tributary of the Limpopo, which sneak around the ridge at Gillooly's Farm and head north to join the Crocodile and Limpopo rivers.

ABOVE: John Ledger's family at the Pafuri picnic site, 1960.

OPPOSITE: The trumpeter hornbill, *Bycanistes bucinator*, with its very distinctive loud call, may be heard or seen from Beit Bridge in the riverine forest through into Mozambique.

PREVIOUS SPREAD: A rowing boat appears out of the misty Limpopo.

In the 1970s we founded the Vulture Study Group, and Peter Norton was one of our champion ringers of Cape vultures when he was a member of the Wits University Mountain Club. We used to gaze upon the waters of the Hartbeespoort Dam on the Crocodile River from the vulture nesting ledges at Skeerpoort in the Magaliesberg.

There are two topics in the book that resonate with my few fleeting affairs with the Limpopo River.

I visited the place where Peter Norton did his parachute jump, and fished in the Limpopo River when he was doing his military training. As Director of the Endangered Wildlife Trust (EWT), Clive Walker had donated a floating trophy for progress in nature conservation to the South African Defence Force – this after he had exposed the involvement of the SADF in rhino and elephant poaching in South West Africa (Namibia). As Clive's successor, I was a member of the judging panel for several awards subsequently put up to encourage the country's armed forces to look after the land under their control. We used to travel around the country to visit various military bases and evaluate the finalists in the different environmental management categories.

We flew to the military base in the Madimbo corridor in a DC3 Dakota (possibly the same one that Peter jumped out of!). We drove around the base and saw the magnificent riverine vegetation on the banks of the Limpopo. A hearty braai followed, and someone suggested a drive to the river to see it under the full moon. Professor Koos Bothma, Chair of Wildlife Management at the University of Pretoria, declined on the grounds of being very tired, and I decided that I had also had enough for the day and retired to bed. We were rudely aroused by the noise of many angry men cursing loudly as they jostled to get into the showers. They had parked on the banks of the Limpopo in a couple of open Land Rovers, admiring the great river glistening in the moonlight, and reminiscing about army days. Above them, in a large fig tree, a troop of roosting baboons grunted and grumbled at the intrusion. Inexplicably, the young soldier driving one of the vehicles blew his hooter. The baboons blew their anal sphincters in unison, and showered the men below with a ghastly rain of baboon bowel broth. I often wondered what happened to that driver …

The other topic that resonates is the story of the Makuleke people, who were evicted from their homes to consolidate the Kruger National Park by taking their land, which stretched to the Limpopo River. From their resettlement villages the Makuleke observed the progress of democracy in South Africa, culminating in the historical handover of power by democratic elections in 1994. They submitted a land claim, and also started training their brightest young people in nature conservation and business management, confident that they would one day manage the land that they had lost.

The EWT renovated a damaged local government building in Ntlaveni village, secured the donation of computer equipment and software, and began a programme to mentor the young students who were studying by correspondence, and not doing too well. An English teacher was sent to Ntlaveni every month, and marks improved dramatically. Many of those young people are now employed as custodians of the magnificent biodiversity reserve along the Limpopo River.

When the long civil war in Mozambique ended in 1992, and that country held its own elections in 1994, it marked the end of a very dark era in the history of southern Africa. During the war the EWT had supported Paul Dutton's conservation work on Bazaruto Island, and on our flights in small aircraft from Maputo to Bazaruto, we looked down on the Limpopo floodplain and its abandoned rice fields, without knowing much about their history or ecology.

If the Limpopo is the golden thread that links us as people, from the plateau to the coast, why don't we treat the river with more respect? We suck the waters up for our agriculture, mines and power stations. We throw our chemicals, used oil and sewage into the golden stream. We build dams to serve our needs, with scant regard for those downstream whose life-blood we are sucking. There is a cliché about the next wars being fought over water, not ideology or religious fanaticism, and that may be true.

But water is remarkable stuff – Dr Anthony Turton refers to it as a 'flux' – that in your own kitchen might exist as a solid, a liquid or a vapour. In an Eskom power station there is another flux – an invisible gas called super-heated steam, which spins the turbines that generate the electricity that drives our modern society. This gas in turn gives up its spent heat to vapour that falls as rain and brings life back to Earth – or could that rain also bring death and destruction back to Earth? The massive periodic floods that the Limpopo unleashes on the unfortunate people of Mozambique are part of the natural global climate system that we understand so poorly.

Thank you to the authors of this wonderful book for pulling together a remarkable account of the history and ecology of this river, which will help future generations understand what has shaped the form and character of the Limpopo that may be grey and greasy one moment, but a massive torrent of water hurtling towards the Indian Ocean the next.

Above all, this book reminds us that a nasty molecule cast carelessly into a little stream in Doornfontein could kill a fish in Xai-Xai and deprive a family of its sustenance. We need to think about that deeply, and look after all our little streams.

Dr John Ledger
Associate Professor of Energy Studies
University of Johannesburg
November 2015

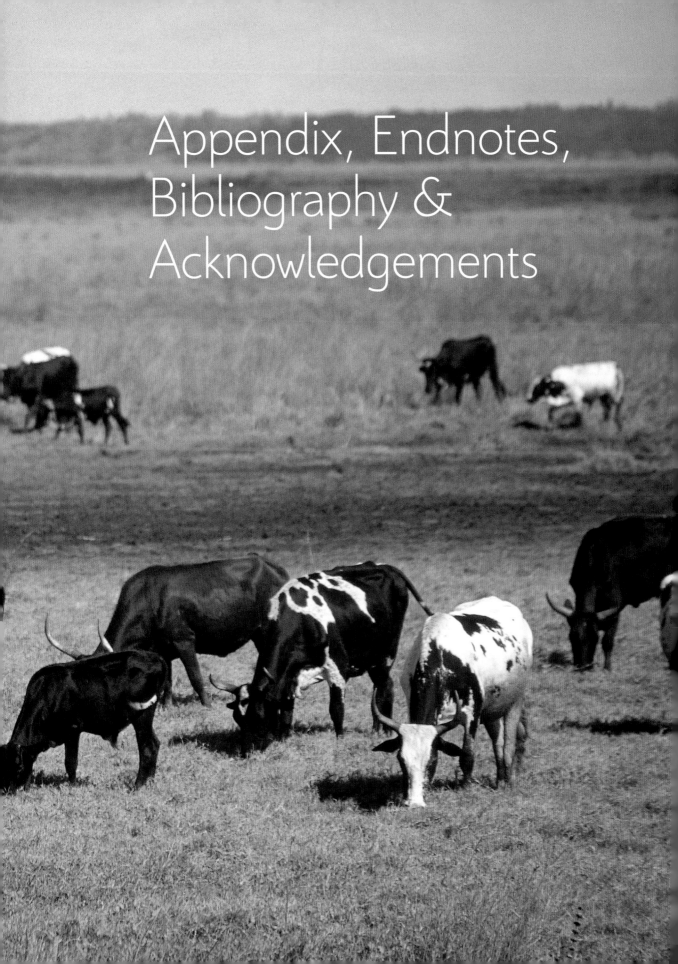

Appendix, Endnotes,
Bibliography &
Acknowledgements

Appendix: The Limpopo Catchment

Catchment Size

In southern African terms the Limpopo can only be considered as a medium-sized river, with a catchment of 415 500 square kilometres. The catchments of the Congo and Zambezi are much larger, and the Orange and Okavango substantially bigger.

Within the Limpopo Basin itself there are four relatively large catchments, the Olifants, Shangane, Crocodile and Shashe; six medium-sized catchments, the Mwenezi, Sand, Umzingwane, Motloutse, Ngotwane and Marico; and a host of smaller catchments.

Topography

The Limpopo River forms a broad arc from the Witwatersrand Highveld around the northern border of South Africa and down to the sea near Xai-Xai in Mozambique.

The watersheds between the Limpopo Basin and neighbouring river basins are the edge of the Zimbabwe Plateau in the north, the slightly higher ground of the Kalahari-Zimbabwe axis in the west, and the Witwatersrand Highveld and Drakensberg in the south.

From the higher ridge of the Witwatersrand, at about 1 700 metres above sea level, the river drops off quite quickly to about 900 metres by Thabazimbi, and then flattens out for 300 kilometres up to near Mmabolela. From there it descends in several steps, interspersed with stretches of relatively flat water. The main steps in the middle and lower part of the river are from Mmabolela to just past the Mogalakwena confluence, the 30 or so kilometres leading up to Beit Bridge (with what Elton calls the Tolo-Azime Waterfall), and the Limpopo Gorge from Malala Drift to Mabaligwe on the Kruger National Park boundary (including what Ramke calls the Malala Falls, the Mahokwe Falls and the Qui-Qui Falls).

Rainfall

The rainfall of southern Africa, particularly south of the Zambezi River generally follows a pattern of increasing aridity (decreasing rainfall) from east to west. The one

OPPOSITE: The African python, *Python sebae*, is a common species along the north-eastern reaches of the river.

PREVIOUS SPREAD: The local Nguni breed of cattle is a common feature of the low-lying floodplains in Mozambique.

exception is the Limpopo Valley, which forms a 'plume' of low rainfall right down the river into Mozambique. This is mostly caused by the fact that the prevailing rain-bearing winds, the south-easterlies, either drop their rain on the coast, and there is no higher ground to cause cooling and the formation of rain clouds in the interior, or else there are mountains such as the Drakensberg Escarpment and the Soutpansberg, which cause all the rain to fall and there is little moisture left in the 'rain shadow' in the Limpopo Valley.

Formation of the River and its Valley[1]

If we want to understand why the Limpopo River follows its particular route to the sea, and to explain some curious characteristics of the river, we need to go right back to the formation of the sub-continent itself. This used to be the unfamiliar territory of esteemed geologists, who speak a language that is unintelligible to us mere mortals. The publication of a recent book entitled *The Story of Earth & Life: A southern African perspective on a 4.6-billion-year journey* has brought the processes forming our sub-continent vividly to life, in an easily understood format. What follows below is a summary of some of the most relevant components.

The Limpopo Belt

An ancient continent formed on the Earth's crust around 3 000 million years ago, made up of plates of material that split and collided. One of the oldest plates, called 'cratons', is now known as the Kaapvaal Craton. It underlies much of southern Africa today and, although buried by other younger sedimentary and volcanic layers several times in the Earth's history, has again been exposed in several areas, including Barberton and along the Limpopo River near Musina. Interestingly, rocks in the Pilbara Region of Western Australia and in portions of Madagascar and India probably also formed part of the Kaapvaal Craton, before the break up of Gondwana.

These ancient rocks are made up of characteristic greenstones and granites, which were formed deep under the Earth's crust and are quite different from the more recent sedimentary and volcanic rocks.

Around 2 700 million years ago another similar micro-continent, the Zimbabwe Craton, collided with the Kaapvaal Craton, rupturing the Earth's crust and allowing vast amounts of lava to erupt. The collision of these continents caused thickening of the crust along their common boundary as sedimentary rocks on the floor of the intervening ocean became compressed between the converging landmasses. These folded rocks were heated and the crust melted, producing granite magmas. The thickened crust formed a mountain range with a deep root, in a manner similar to the modern Himalayan range, which formed as a result of the (much younger) collision of India with Asia.

The mountain range resulting from the collision of the two continents was rapidly eroded, causing the rise of its root zone, with the result that rocks previously buried to a depth of at least 30 kilometres in the crust became exposed on the surface.

'Today, minerals characteristically formed at very high temperatures and pressures (metamorphic rocks) occur in the rocks on the surface along the Limpopo River. These rocks form a linear zone, known as the Limpopo Belt, along the boundary between the two formerly separate continents, and mark the suture between the two continents. It is difficult to imagine that the hot, flat and monotonous country north of the Soutpansberg was once the site of snow-covered peaks like the Himalaya, but the geological evidence indicates that such a range certainly did exist'.[2]

Three-way Split at Crooks' Corner

About 180 million years ago, a mantle plume (a hot, buoyant mass of molten rock that rises from deep within the Earth to below the crust) is believed to have risen beneath what is today southern Mozambique, generating extensive volcanic activity over southern Africa and neighbouring parts of Gondwana. The widespread distribution of Drakensberg and related basalts was a product of this volcanism. The same mantle plume was probably also responsible for initiating the opening of the Indian Ocean.

Mantle plumes beneath continents may cause rifting along three axes arranged at 120° to one another. McCarthy and Rubidge suggest that the mantle plume was situated at approximately Crooks' Corner, with one rift southwards along the Lebombo mountains, a second north-eastwards along the base of the Chimanimani mountains, and a third north-westwards into the Limpopo Valley. Unlike the East African Rift Valley, which also probably arose from a mantle plume that formed the Red Sea and the Gulf of Aden, this third rift did not open up further, but its initial development would later form the drainage line of the Limpopo River from Crooks' Corner to the Shashe confluence.

The vast amounts of sediment brought down by the proto-Limpopo River (which at that time included most of the catchment of today's Zambezi River) formed a huge delta at the river mouth – that rounded bulge on the coast between Maputo and Beira, with the centre of the fan around the Bazaruto Islands. Later, minor tilting of the crust, or differences in hardness of the sediments probably caused the river to find a more southerly route to its present position with a mouth at Xai-Xai.

The Shashe–Zambezi Link

Thus, in the period following the break-up of Gondwana, the river systems from the Angolan Highlands drained towards the east, and followed the Limpopo Valley, to the sea. So *all* of the major rivers, the Upper Zambezi, the Kwando, the Quito and the Cubango, drained via what is now the Shashe, and to some extent the Motloutse into the Limpopo. This explains why the present Shashe River is so much wider than the Limpopo at the Limpopo–Shashe confluence.

In those days the confluence of these two mighty rivers must have been a truly awesome sight, with huge volumes of water flowing past what would much later become Mapungubwe to the sea. In fact that part of the Limpopo flowing in from the south, from the confluence of the Crocodile and Marico rivers, would have been a relatively minor tributary: the real Limpopo River of those times flowed from the north-west.

About 60 million years ago the interior of the African continent became gently arched over a number of axes, one of which, the Kalahari–Zimbabwe axis, running from north-east to south-west, cut off the headwaters of the Limpopo; as a result, large lakes began to form in the interior, notably Lake Makgadikgadi. Then about 14 million years ago the East African Rift System began to propagate southwards into southern Africa, gradually capturing first the Kafue, then the Upper Zambezi, then the Kwando, causing them to feed into the Lower Zambezi System (and creating, in the process, both the Okavango Delta and the Victoria Falls). The consequence of this 'capture' by the Zambezi was that the flow into the Limpopo via the Shashe was hugely reduced, but it left behind a wide Shashe riverbed, and a massive alluvial fan from Xai-Xai to Beira on the Mozambique coast.

Rock Formations

In the aeon that passed between the collision of the Kaapvaal and Zimbabwe cratons and the beginning of the break-up of Gondwana, the metamorphic rocks of the Limpopo Belt became covered in many areas by sedimentary rocks (and lavas) of younger events, especially those of the Transvaal and Karoo Supergroups (at around 2 000 and 200 million years ago respectively); in between, by the formation of the Waterberg and Soutpansberg ranges at around 1 700 million years ago; and in the last 50 million years by Kalahari sands. More recently, many of these younger deposits have themselves been eroded, to expose once again the granites and gneisses that are so characteristic of the modern Limpopo riverbed. Some remnants of these events remain of course, notably the deposits of Karoo-age coal-rich shales that straddle the Limpopo between Lephalale in South Africa and Mmamabula in Botswana; and other, smaller coal deposits like the controversial one immediately downstream from Mapungubwe. But given time, these rocks too will find themselves eroded and transported inexorably to the sea by the Limpopo or its successors.

Habitats

Under the influence of differences in landscape or topography, rainfall, river flow, drainage and soil type, a wide diversity of habitats occurs in the Limpopo Basin leading to a great diversity of plant and animal species.

The Limpopo River only flows through two biomes (major regional ecological communities): the Grassland Biome and the Savanna Biome. However, within these biomes there is rich diversity at a smaller scale. In particular, the rocky ridges and koppies that are so characteristic of some sections of the river often house a biodiversity that is very different from the surrounding plains.

Alongside the river itself the underground water tends to support a riverine forest that is much higher and greener than the surrounding veld. The large trees are very much part of the mystique of the Limpopo River, particularly the huge sycamore figs (*Ficus sycomorus*), ana trees (*Faidherbia albida* – formerly Acacia), mashatu or nyala-berry (*Xanthocercis zambesiacus*) and the ever-present fever-trees (*Acacia xanthophloea*).

Lesser drainages have the rain tree (*Lonchocarpus capassa*) and leadwood (*Combretum imberbe*), the wood of the latter having been the preferred wood to burn in myriad campfires along the Limpopo River.

Throughout the Bushveld from just before Olifants Drift onwards, stately baobabs (*Adansonia digitata*) become a key feature of the landscape, all the way to Macarretane in Mozambique. If one had to select a single tree that captures the essence of the Limpopo Valley, it would have to be the baobab, presiding over a range of Mopane and Mixed Bushveld habitats.

In the Limpopo National Park of Mozambique, the Mopane Bushveld continues as far as the Olifants River confluence, with sweeter Mixed Bushveld in the south-western areas. From just before Combomune onwards, there is an abrupt change in the quality of the alluvial soil, and the Limpopo floodplain is almost completely converted to agriculture or grassland used for grazing cattle, all the way to the sea. From about Macarretane the floodplain fans out to a considerable distance from the river, and here the habitat is some of the original Mixed Bushveld interspersed with cleared agricultural lands, and the planting of exotic cashew nut trees. In the last few kilometres before the mouth, there are well-developed mangrove forests.

Birdwatching on the Limpopo

The rich variety of habitats support an extraordinary variety of birdlife, and birdwatching is one of the fastest growing forms of tourism in the Limpopo Valley. The Soutpansberg-Limpopo Birding Route (SLBR) established in 2003 has spawned several other birding routes, grouped under the Greater-Limpopo Birding Routes[3] and Limpopo Province is using Birding Special Interest Tourism as a key focus for tourism development in the province. Lodges in state and private nature reserves, such as Northern Tuli Game Reserve, Mapungubwe National Park and the Pafuri region of Kruger National Park have reported substantial growth and interest in birdwatching among their guests, and progress is being made with using avi-tourism as a catalyst for rural socio-economic development.

The SLBR boasts 29 southern African endemics and 32 southern African near-endemics, with a total of over 400 resident species, as well as about 180 migrants. A number of 'specials' can be seen at a range of sites in the middle and lower Limpopo Valley (see table below).[4]

Top 10 birds for the SLBR
(resident species that cannot be found elsewhere in South Africa)
Tropical Boubou
Senegal Coucal
Three-banded Courser
Southern Hyliota
Dickinson's Kestrel
Grey-headed Parrot
Bōhm's Spinetail
Mottled Spinetail
Meves's Starling
Blue-spotted Wood-Dove

Regional Specials
(uncommon elsewhere in South Africa, but relatively easy to find in SLBR)
African Broadbill
Kori Bustard
Lemon-breasted Canary
Arnot's Chat
Blue-mantled Crested-Flycatcher
African Mourning Dove
Pel's Fishing-Owl
Southern Ground-Hornbill
Orange Ground-Thrush
Crested Guineafowl
Crowned Hornbill
Dusky Lark
Eastern Nicator
White-backed Night-Heron
Meyer's Parrot
Broad-billed Roller
Mosque Swallow
Pink-throated Twinspot
Black-throated Wattle-eye
Olive Woodpecker

Regional Non-Resident Specials
(uncommon elsewhere in South
Africa, but found here in the
summer months)
Southern Carmine Bee-eater
Black Coucal
Grey-headed Kingfisher
Lesser Moorhen
Thrush Nightingale
Pennant-winged Nightjar
African Golden Oriole
Eurasian Golden Oriole
Green Sandpiper
Olive-tree Warbler

Regional Raptor Specials
Bateleur
Forest Buzzard
African Crowned Eagle
Lesser Spotted Eagle
Steppe Eagle
Dark Chanting Goshawk
Montagu's Harrier
Pallid Harrier
Ayres's Hawk-Eagle
Hooded Vulture
Rüppell's Vulture
White-headed Vulture

BELOW: The African fish-eagle, *Haliaeetus vocifer*, may be seen along the entire length of the river from just north of Johannesburg to the mouth on the Indian Ocean.

Wildlife of the Limpopo

The big game, particularly the Big Five – lion, leopard, elephant, both species of rhino and buffalo, and one can add the hippo – used to be common throughout the Limpopo Valley, but were largely hunted out long ago, and now only occur in selected large state- and privately-owned nature reserves where a number have been reintroduced. The Northern and Southern Tuli game reserves comprise the largest free-ranging population of elephant on private land. The hippo fortunately survived in sections of the river. There are many stories of encounters with them in this book.

The second category is the larger species that have managed to survive right up to modern times. The most obvious candidates here are the snakes and crocodiles. Snakes are present throughout the length of the river, and are clearly a factor in the bush, for which careful precautions and provision for emergencies should be taken.

If one were to choose one large and dangerous animal that is most clearly associated with the Limpopo River, it would have to be the crocodile. Most accounts of explorers, hunters, naturalists, canoeists, and other adventurers include at least some mention of crocodiles, and the possibility of being attacked right into the twenty-first century at the same time terrifies and thrills.

If anyone thought that crocodiles were a thing of the past, except in major parks, the recent death of an American tourist taken out of a canoe in the Tuli Section of the Limpopo River proves that large and aggressive crocodiles are very much part of the river.

In the same category as the crocodile would be sharks. They are still found well up from the Limpopo Mouth, and Van Riet recounts his canoe being attacked right up at Guija, nearly 200 kilometres from the sea (see box on page 38). Even more remarkable was the Zambezi shark that was caught up at Crooks' Corner, nearly 600 kilometres by river from the coast! This would not happen again, because the Macarretane Barrage would be an insurmountable barrier for sharks.

The third category is the more insidious and less visible type of dangerous animal, that includes scorpions, tsetse flies and malaria mosquitoes. Because of its importance in determining historical movements of people – and most of us do not know much about it because it is no longer a threat – the tsetse fly is dealt with in more detail in the next section. In contrast, malaria is well-known, and most visitors to the Limpopo Valley downstream of Musina take some form of precaution.

Tsetse Fly[5]

Before 1890 the tsetse fly, which carries horse-sickness or *nagana*, occurred in a wide arc of the Limpopo Valley and South African Lowveld from northern Zululand, right up along the base of the Drakensberg escarpment, and arcing round up the Limpopo Valley almost as far as Rustenburg. In fact, it was two main species that occurred, *Glossina morsitans* in the Limpopo Valley, and G.*pallidipes* in Zululand, with several other species occurring in various areas of the sub-continent.

The type specimen (the specimen that was first scientifically described) of *Glossina morsitans* was collected by Frank Vardon, who accompanied W Cotton Oswell on a hunting trip to the Limpopo in 1846, on some low hills that he named the Siloquano Hills.

In these days of rapid, motorised transport, mosquito nets, malaria pills/sprays and creams, it is difficult for us to imagine just how daunting the Lowveld must have been to the early travellers. Not only was malaria widespread, without the prophylactics and cures we have today, but the tsetse fly was found almost throughout a wide belt.

For anybody who ventured into the Limpopo Valley Lowveld up to the late 1800s, there was a good chance that most of their oxen and horses would die within a few weeks, and some of their party would die from malaria soon after. This is what happened to Louis Trichardt and his trek, who managed to make their way to Delagoa Bay, but lost most of their horses, cattle and small stock on the way, which must have been devastating to people who were so dependent on their animals. To cap it all, after struggling into Delagoa Bay most of the party, including Trichardt himself, then died of malaria.

Another person to suffer major losses from tsetse flies was R Gordon-Cumming, on his hunting trip down the Limpopo in 1846. His horses and cattle were bitten by tsetse flies, probably at Seleka's Kop in Botswana, 15 kilometres north-west of the

Lephalala confluence. Within a few weeks he had just the last one out of 15 horses left, and all except two of his several spans of oxen had died from the tsetse.[6] He had to get help from Dr David Livingstone who sent teams of oxen to take their wagons to Kolobeng.

Tsetse fly do not appear to have occurred everywhere, but rather in 'belts' related to thicket and bush habitat. This meant that it was possible for people to navigate through the 'tsetse area', as was done by Thomas Baines in 1871 when returning along the Nylstroom/Mogalakwena at the request of Lobengula. He was accompanied by *indunas* from the Matabele king who guided him through the tsetse areas, often by travelling at night or in bad weather, and Baines reached the Highveld with no losses at all.

Another traveller who survived the tsetse threat was Captain Frederick Elton, who used three pack oxen after his boat was destroyed at the Tolo-Azime Falls, and, although one was lost in a bog, the other two lasted all the way to Delagoa Bay.

Many writers have reported that one benefit of the devastating rinderpest epidemic of 1896 was that the tsetse fly was virtually wiped out in southern Africa at the same time. However, there is substantial evidence that the fly had disappeared from the whole of the Limpopo Valley as far as Malala Drift before 1890, probably by 1888. This may have been due to heavy hunting of wildlife in the valley up to this period, to the point where most of the larger herbivores had been exterminated.

After the rinderpest the tsetse had disappeared from the whole Limpopo Valley and, indeed, from southern Africa south of the Zambezi, apart from a small pocket in Zululand. This allowed much freer travelling on horseback and by ox wagon, and various groups moved into areas such as the middle Limpopo Valley to start cattle ranching where it had never been possible to farm with cattle before.

Fish and Fishing

There are 50 fish species found in the Limpopo River System. This is 28 per cent of all South Africa's fish species, compared to the Pongola River which has only 40 species; the Tugela has 12 species; and the Orange River has only 16 species.

Despite the central role of the river in people's lives, fishing is relatively unimportant for local populations in most of the Limpopo Basin, particularly in Zimbabwe, Botswana and to some degree South Africa. The wide variability in river levels and temperature, as well as the occurrence of prolonged dry spells, means that the river has few species and normally small fish populations.

However, the Mozambican inhabitants of the Limpopo Basin benefit more significantly from fishing. River fishing makes an important contribution to households, either by generating monetary income or for household consumption in some parts of the basin. Not surprisingly the coast is where fishing is most important. The river's flow increases the productivity of coastal swamps, were fish and shrimp spawn. In the Bilene district the trade in dried fish in exchange for produce and cereals from the interior of Chibuto is an important part of the local economy.

The annual production of fish in the Massingir Reservoir is more than 500 tonnes, and the dam may have considerable potential for further fisheries development. Recent tourism studies have emphasised the potential for sport fishing.

Tigerfish are found in the Luvuvhu River, as well as in the Okavango and Upper Zambezi, but not in any of the coastal rivers in between. This again supports the concept of a direct linkage between the Okavango and Upper Zambezi with the Limpopo.

Cattle

A book on the Limpopo area would not be complete without at least a brief mention of cattle. Cattle are so central to the history and the livelihoods of many of the people of the Limpopo, and such a feature of the landscape in rural areas, that they cannot be ignored.

Cattle, together with seeds of seed crops, were the key resource that migrating people took with them. They were useful as a means of ploughing, transport (sleds and bullock carts), storage of wealth for drought years, and payment of *lobola* (especially in the Nguni-based southern areas of Mozambique).

Cattle kraals were the focal point of the lives of many of the early inhabitants of the Limpopo Valley and therefore the basic layout of homesteads throughout the area is known as the 'Central Cattle Pattern'. This remained relatively unchanged until the pattern of Ritual Seclusion of the Sacred Leader introduced by the Mapungubwe Kingdom came along.

In recent decades the cattle herds of Mozambique were devastated by the combined effects of war and drought. The total reached a peak of 1.4 million in 1975, just before independence, but reduced to 300 000 in 1992. Since then there have been government-led restocking programmes.

Website details of NGOs involved in river, wetlands and biodiversity conservation:

www.birdlife.org.za   www.wessa.org.za
www.ewt.org.za   www.wwf.org.za
www.ppf.org.za

Endnotes

Chapter 1

1 Birkby, C. 1939. *Limpopo Journey*. London: Muller.
2 Harris, W Cornwallis. 1986 *Portraits of the Game and Wild Animals of Southern Africa*. Alberton: Galago Publishing.
3 Erskine, St Vincent. 1869. 'Journey of exploration to the mouth of the River Limpopo'. *Journal of the Royal Geographical Society* 39: 250.
4 Erskine, St Vincent. 1875. 'A Journey to Umzila's, South Eastern Africa'. *Journal of the Royal Geographical Society* 45: 110–134.
5 Ferreira, OJO. 2002. *Montanha in Soutpansberg: 'n Portugese handelsending van Inhambane se besoek aan Schoemansdal, 1855–1856*. Pretoria: Protea Boekhuis, PMN translation.
6 Ralushai, NMN. 2001. Preliminary report on the oral history of the Mapungubwe area. Unpublished report for Department of Environmental Affairs and Tourism, Pretoria, pp. 23–24.
7 Wheatcroft, G. 1985. *The Randlords: South Africa's robber barons and the mines that forged a nation*. New York: Simon & Schuster.
8 Erskine. 1869.
9 Carruthers, J. Undated. 'Placing "elephants for want of towns": Mapping the Transvaal environment, *c*.1860–1899'. Unpublished manuscript, p. 7.
10 Bosman, HC. 1947. *Mafeking Road*. Cape Town: Human & Rousseau.
11 Kipling, R. 1902. *Just So Stories*. Reprinted in 1953. London: Macmillan.
12 Wilson, A. 1979. *The Strange Ride of Rudyard Kipling: His life and works*. London: Granada.
13 Battiss, W. 1965. *Limpopo*. Pretoria: Van Schaik.
14 Elton, F. 1873. 'Journal of an exploration of the Limpopo River'. *Journal of the Royal Geographical Society*, Vol XLII: 1–47.
15 Ramke. In prep. '"Our Family" The Saga of the Ramke-Meyer/Southey and Mclachlan/Hurley Families in South Africa'.
16 Van Riet, W. 1966. *Stroom af in my Kano: Avonture op Vyf Groot Riviere in Suider-Afrika*. Cape Town: Tafelberg.
17 Personal communication with Sean Waller in 2006.
18 For further information about Robert Perkins's film, go to www.gotrob.com.

Chapter 2

1 This information comes from the Constitution Hill website www.constitutionhill.org.za.
2 www.constitutionhill.org.za.
3 St Mary's Cathedral. 1992. 'The Cathedral Chapel of St Mary on the Limpopo'. *The Parishioner*, March.
4 Gauteng Department of Agriculture, Conservation, Environment & Land. 2002. *Bronberg Strategic Environmental Assessment*. Gauteng: GDACEL.
5 Gauteng Provincial Government Department of Agriculture, Conservation and Environment. 1998. *Application for Inclusion on the World Heritage List: The Fossil Hominid Sites of Sterkfontein, Swartkrans, Kromdraai and Environs, South Africa*. Johannesburg: Gauteng Provincial Government.
6 Harris, W Cornwallis. 1986. *Portraits of the Game and Wild Animals of Southern Africa*. London for the proprietor. Alberton: Galago Publishing.
7 Vincent Carruthers, personal communication to Clive Walker, July 2015.
8 MacKenzie, R. 1993. *David Livingstone: The truth behind the legend*. Zimbabwe: Fig Tree.
9 *Dictionary of South African Bibliography*. 1968. Pretoria: National Council for Social Research.
10 Coetzee, TA. 1987. *Thabazimbi: Gister en Vandag*. 123pp.
11 Hickman, AS. 1970. *Rhodesia Served the Queen*. Salisbury: Govt. Printer.

Chapter 3

1 Hall, M. 1987. *The Changing Past: Farmers, kings and traders in southern Africa, 200–1860*. Cape Town: David Philip

2 Cumming, RG. 1850. *A Hunter's Life in South Africa*. Reprinted 1986. Alberton: Galago, pp. 295–298.

3 Hall, G. 2003. The Archaeology of Mashatu. 5pp. A compendium of archaeological sites and artifacts from Mashatu Game Reserve. Johannesburg.

4 Fry, E. 1891. *Occupation of Mashonaland*. Reprinted in 1982. Bulawayo: Books of Zimbabwe; Leonard, AG. 1896. *How We Made Rhodesia*. London: Keagan, Paul, Trench, Trubner; Walker, C. 1992. *Dear Elephant Sir*. Johannesburg: Southern Book.

5 Zeederberg, H. 1971. *Veld Express*. Cape Town: Howard Timmins; De la Harpe, R & P. 2004. *Tuli – land of giants*. Cape Town: Sunbird; Walker, 1992. *Dear Elephant Sir*.

6 Gilfillan, AD. Undated. 'The Boer and British engagements in the Eastern Tuli Area and the significance thereof with regard to the outcome of the Second Anglo Boer War of 1899–1902'. Unpublished; Hickman, AS. 1970. *Rhodesia Served the Queen*. Salisbury: Govt. Printer.

7 Bulpin, TV. 1965. *Lost Trails of the Transvaal*. Cape Town: Howard Timmins; Baines, T. 1877. *The Gold Regions of S.E. Africa*. Reprinted in 1968. Bulawayo: Books of Rhodesia.

8 Bull, B. 1992. *Safari: A chronicle of adventure*. London: Penguin.

9 The first edition of Harris, W Cornwallis. *The Wild Sports of Southern Africa*, was actually published in Bombay in 1838, under a different title, but the second edition with this title was published in England in 1839.

10 Cumming, 1850. *A Hunter's Life*.

Chapter 4

1 Most of the information for this section comes from the Mapungubwe World Heritage Site Nomination prepared for the Department of Environmental Affairs & Tourism in 2002; and Huffman, TN. 2005. *Mapungubwe: Ancient African Civilisation on the Limpopo*. Johannesburg: Wits University Press.

2 Carruthers, J. 1992. 'The Dongola Wild Life Sanctuary: "Psychological blunder, economic folly and political monstrosity" or "More valuable than rubies and gold"?' *Kleio* XXIV.

3 Ralushai, NMN. 2005. *Oral History of the Mapungubwe*. Unpublished manuscript.

4 Huffman, 2005. *Mapungubwe*.

Chapter 5

1 Hennop, E. 2001. 'SANDF Control of the North-Eastern Border Areas of South Africa'. Institute for Security Studies, Occasional Paper No. 52, August.

2 Ralushai, NMN. 2001. Preliminary report on the oral history of the Mapungubwe area. Unpublished report for Dept of Environmental Affairs and Tourism, Pretoria.

3 Wongtschowski, BEH. 1990. *Between Woodbush and Wolkberg: Googoo Thompson's story*. 2nd Edn. Self-published.

4 Wongtschowski, 1990. *Between Woodbush and Wolkberg*.

5 Wheatcroft, G. 1985. *The Randlords: South Africa's robber barons and the mines that forged a nation*. New York: Simon & Schuster.

6 Van Riet, W. 1966. *Stroom af in my Kano: Avonture op Vyf Groot Riviere in Suider-Afrika*. Cape Town: Tafelberg

7 Norton, PM. 1971. Unpublished army diary.

8 Linden, T. 2004. Land and conflict in the Madimbo Corridor: seminar for TPARI. Available from: www.hdgc.epp.cmu.edu/misc/Thema%20Linden.pdf.

9 Deacon, AR. 1996. Limpopo/Luvuvhu River Floodplains and Pans: RAMSAR Data.

10 Koch, E. 2003. The Makuleke Region of the Kruger National Park: Community led partnerships for conservation and development. Unpublished.

11 Bulpin, TV. 1955. *The Ivory Trail*. Cape Town: Howard Timmins.

12 Pienaar, U de V. (ed). 1990. *Neem uit die verlede*. Pretoria: National Parks Board.
13 Pienaar, (ed). 1990. *Neem uit die verlede*.

Chapter 6
1 Pienaar, U de V. (ed). 1990. *Neem uit die verlede*. Pretoria: National Parks Board.
2 Erskine, St Vincent. 1875a: 110–134.
3 Wheeler, Douglas L. 1968. Gungunyane the negotiator: a study in African diplomacy. *Journal of African History* 9: 583–602; Newitt, M. 1995. *A History of Mozambique*. Bloomington & Indianapolis: Indiana University Press.
4 Coetzee, FP. 2003. 'Archaeological predictive assessment: Limpopo National Park, Mozambique'. Unpublished report.
5 Ferreira, OJO. 2002. *Montanha in Soutpansberg: 'n Portugese handelsending van Inhambane se besoek aan Schoemansdal, 1855–1856*. Pretoria: Protea Boekhuis.
6 An overview of the state of mapping of the Limpopo is given in Carruthers, J. Undated. 'Placing "elephants for want of towns": Mapping the Transvaal environment, c.1860–1899'. Unpublished manuscript.
7 Erskine, St Vincent. 1869. 'Journey of exploration to the mouth of the River Limpopo'. *Journal of the Royal Geographical Society* 39: 233–276.
8 Erskine, St Vincent. 1875a. 'A Journey to Umzila's, South Eastern Africa'. *Journal of the Royal Geographical Society* 45: 110–134.
9 *Atlas for Disaster Preparedness and Response in the Limpopo Basin*. 2003. INGC, UEM-Department of Geography and FEWS NET MIND.
10 Bowen, Merle L. 1989. 'Peasant agriculture in Mozambique: The case of Chokwe, Gaza Province'. *Canadian Journal of African Studies* 23: 355–379.
11 Newitt, 1995. *A History of Mozambique*.
12 Forand, M. 2005. Lighthouse development in Mozambique, 1908–1931. Available from: www.unc.edu/~rowlett/lighthouse/resources/moz/index.htm.
13 Newitt, 1995. *A History of Mozambique*; Briggs, Philip. 2014. *Mozambique*.

Appendix
1 McCarthy, T & Rubidge, B. 2005. *The Story of Earth and Life: A southern African perspective on a 4.6-billion-year journey*. Cape Town: Struik.
2 McCarthy & Rubidge, 2005. *The Story of Earth and Life*, p. 111.
3 Venter, S, Grosel, J & De Boer, B. 2006. *Greater Limpopo Birding Self-drive Routes*. 4th Edn. BirdlifeSA. Pamphlet/map.
4 Wadley, R. 2015. Geology notes. Personal communication.
5 Fuller, C. 1923. 'Tsetse Fly in the Transvaal and Surrounding Territories: An historical overview'. Union of South Africa, *Department of Agriculture Entomology Memoirs*. Memoir No. 3. Pretoria.
6 Cumming, RG. 1850. *A Hunter's Life in South Africa*. Reprinted 1986. Alberton: Galago, pp. 337–339.

Bibliography

Atlas for Disaster Preparedness and Response in the Limpopo Basin. 2003. INGC, UEM-Department of Geography and FEWS NET MIND.
Baines, T. 1854. 'The Limpopo, its origin, course and tributaries'. *Journal of the Royal Society* 24: 288–291.
Baines, T. 1877. *The Gold Regions of S.E. Africa*. Reprinted in 1968. Bulawayo: Books of Rhodesia.
Battiss, W. 1965. *Limpopo*. Pretoria: Van Schaik.
Birkby, C. 1939. *Limpopo Journey*. London: Muller.

Bodman, W. 1981. *The North Flowing Rivers of the Central Witwatersrand: A visual survey*. 15pp.

Bonner, P. & Carruthers, EJ. 2003. The recent history of the Mapungubwe area. Unpublished report, Dept of Environmental Affairs & Tourism.

Bosman, HC. 1947. *Mafeking Road*. Cape Town: Human & Rousseau.

Bowen, Merle L. 1989. 'Peasant agriculture in Mozambique: The case of Chokwe, Gaza Province'. *Canadian Journal of African Studies* 23: 355–379.

Briggs, Philip. 2014. *Mozambique*. 6th Edition. UK: Bradt Travel Guides.

Buchan, J. 1903. *The African Colony: Studies in the reconstruction*. Edinburgh: Blackwood, MCM III.

Bull, B. 1992. *Safari: A chronicle of adventure*. London: Penguin.

Bulpin, TV. 1955. *The Ivory Trail*. Cape Town: Howard Timmins.

Bulpin, TV. 1965. *Lost Trails of the Transvaal*. Cape Town: Howard Timmins.

Carruthers, J. 1992. 'The Dongola Wild Life Sanctuary: "Psychological blunder, economic folly and political monstrosity" or "More valuable than rubies and gold"?' *Kleio* XXIV.

Carruthers, J. Undated. 'Placing "elephants for want of towns": Mapping the Transvaal environment, *c*.1860–1899'. Unpublished manuscript.

Carruthers, V. 1990. *The Magaliesberg*. Pretoria: Protea.

Cattrick, A. 1959. *Spoor of Blood*. Cape Town: Howard Timmins.

Christie, Sean. 'Searching for the soul of the Jukskei'. *Mail & Guardian*. 3 January 2014.

Coetzee, FP. 2003. 'Archaeological predictive assessment: Limpopo National Park, Mozambique'. Unpublished report.

Coetzee, TA. 1987. *Thabazimbi: Gister en Vandag*. 123pp.

Cumming, RG. 1850. *A Hunter's Life in South Africa*. Reprinted 1986. Alberton: Galago.

Deacon, AR. 1996. Limpopo/Luvuvhu River Floodplains and Pans: RAMSAR Data.

De la Harpe, R & P. 2004. *Tuli – land of giants*. Cape Town: Sunbird.

Department of Environmental Affairs & Tourism. 2002. Mapungubwe World Heritage Site Nomination. Unpublished report.

Dictionary of South African Bibliography. 1968. Pretoria: National Council for Social Research Pretoria.

Dirapeng (Pty) Ltd. Undated. *Madikwe Game Reserve*. 16pp. Available from: whoswho.co.za/dirapeng-Pty-Ltd-7431.

Eastwood, E. 2001. 'The rock art of the Limpop-Shashe Confluence Area. A contribution towards national and world heritage site status for the Mapungubwe area'. Unpublished report for the Department of Environmental Affairs and Tourism.

Eastwood, E & C. 2006. *Capturing the Spoor: An exploration of the rock art of northernmost South Africa*. Cape Town: David Philip.

Elton, F. 1873. 'Journal of an exploration of the Limpopo River'. *Journal of the Royal Geographical Society*, Vol XLII: 1–47.

Emery, MA. 1977. *The Bend in the River: Adventures on a Limpopo Ranch*. Sandton: self-published.

Erskine, St Vincent. 1869. 'Journey of exploration to the mouth of the River Limpopo'. *Journal of the Royal Geographical Society* 39: 233–276.

Erskine, St Vincent. 1875. 'A Journey to Umzila's, South Eastern Africa'. *Journal of the Royal Geographical Society* 45: 110–134.

Erskine, St Vincent. 1878. 'Third and fourth journeys in Gaza, or Southern Mozambique'. *Journal of the Royal Geographic Society* 48: 25–56.

Ferreira, OJO. 2002. *Montanha in Soutpansberg: 'n Portugese handelsending van Inhambane se besoek aan Schoemansdal, 1855–1856*. Pretoria: Protea Boekhuis.

Finnaughty, W. 1980. *The Recollections of an Elephant Hunter 1864–1875*. Bulawayo: Books of Zimbabwe.

Forand, M. 2005. Lighthouse development in Mozambique, 1908–1931. Available from: www.unc.edu/~rowlett/lighthouse/resources/moz/index.htm.

Fry, E. 1891. *Occupation of Mashonaland*. Reprinted in 1982. Bulawayo: Books of Zimbabwe.

Fuller, C. 1923. 'Tsetse Fly in the Transvaal and Surrounding Territories: An historical overview'. Union of South Africa, *Department of Agriculture Entomology Memoirs*. Memoir No. 3. Pretoria.

Gauteng Department of Agriculture, Conservation, Environment & Land. 2002. *Bronberg Strategic Environmental Assessment*.

Gauteng Provincial Government Department of Agriculture, Conservation and Environment. 1998. *Application for Inclusion on the World Heritage List: The Fossil Hominid Sites of Sterkfontein, Swartkrans, Kromdraai and Environs, South Africa*. Johannesburg: Gauteng Provincial Government.

Gilfillan, AD. Undated. 'The Boer and British engagements in the Eastern Tuli Area and the significance thereof with regard to the outcome of the Second Anglo Boer War of 1899–1902'. Unpublished.

Hall, G. 2003. The Archaeology of Mashatu. 5pp. A compendium of archaeological sites and artifacts from Mashatu Game Reserve. Johannesburg.

Hall, M. 1987. *The Changing Past: Farmers, kings and traders in southern Africa, 200–1860*. Cape Town: David Philip.

Hall-Martin, A & Lorimer, RJ. 1995. Limpopo Valley Conservation Area. Unpublished report, National Parks Board.

Harris, W Cornwallis. 1986. *Portraits of the Game and Wild Animals of Southern Africa*. Alberton: Galago Publishing. 1986.

Harris, W Cornwallis. 1852. *The Wild Sports of Southern Africa*. 5th Edn. London: Bohn.

Hennop, E. 2001. 'SANDF Control of the North-Eastern Border Areas of South Africa'. Institute for Security Studies, Occasional Paper No. 52, August.

Hickman, AS. 1970. *Rhodesia Served the Queen*. Salisbury: Govt. Printer.

Hilton-Barber, B & Berger, LR. 2002. *The Official Guide to the Cradle of Humankind: Sterkfontein, Swartkrans, Kromdraai & Environs World Heritage Site*. Cape Town: Struik.

Huffman, TN. 2005. *Mapungubwe: Ancient African Civilisation on the Limpopo*. Johannesburg: Wits University Press.

Kipling, R. 1902. *Just So Stories*. Reprinted in 1953. London: Macmillan.

Koch, E. 2003. The Makuleke Region of the Kruger National Park: Community led partnerships for conservation and development. Unpublished.

Leonard, AG. 1896. *How We Made Rhodesia*. London: Keagan, Paul, Trench, Trubner.

Leslie, M & Maggs, T (eds). 2000. *African Naissance: The Limpopo Valley 1000 years ago*. The South African Archaeological Society Goodwin Series Vol 8.

Lind, P. 'Shashe Limpopo Ranger Report, 1973/74'. Unpublished.

Linden, T. 2004. Land and conflict in the Madimbo Corridor: seminar for TPARI. Available from: hdgc.epp.cmu.edu/misc/Thema%20Linden.pdf.

Mahube Consortium. 2003. Cradle of Humankind World Heritage Site. Cultural Heritage Resources Survey. Unpublished report, Gauteng Dept of Agriculture, Conservation, Environment and Land Affairs.

MacKenzie, R. 1993. *David Livingstone: The truth behind the legend*. Zimbabwe: Fig Tree.

McCarthy, T & Rubidge, B. 2005. *The Story of Earth and Life: A southern African perspective on a 4.6-billion-year journey*. Cape Town: Struik.

Montgomery, DSH. 1992. *Two Shores of the Ocean*. Hanley Swan, Worcestershire: Malvern.

Mucina, L, Rutherford, MC & Powrie, LW (eds). 2005. *Vegetation Map of South Africa, Lesotho and Swaziland*. Pretoria: SA National Botanical Institute.

Newitt, M. 1995. *A History of Mozambique*. Bloomington & Indianapolis: Indiana University Press.

Norton, PM. 1971. Unpublished army diary.

Parsons, N. 1980. *Settlement in east-central Botswana, c.1800–1920*. Paper presented at the 'Settlement in Botswana' symposium. The Botswana Society. 1982.

Pienaar, U de V. (ed). 1990. *Neem uit die verlede*. Pretoria: National Parks Board.

Poland, M, Hammond-Tooke, D & Voight, L. 2003. *The Abundant Herds: A Celebration of the Cattle of the Zulu People*. Cape Town: Fernwood.

Ralushai, NMN. 2001. Preliminary report on the oral history of the Mapungubwe area. Unpublished report for Dept of Environmental Affairs and Tourism, Pretoria.

Ralushai, NMN. 2005. *Oral History of the Mapungubwe*. Unpublished manuscript.

Ramke. In prep. '"Our Family" The Saga of the Ramke-Meyer/Southey and Mclachlan/Hurley Families in South Africa'.

Selous, FC. 1893. *Travel & Adventure in South East Africa*. Reprinted in 1972. Bulawayo: Books of Rhodesia.

Sinclair, I. 2002. *Sasol Birds of Southern Africa*. Cape Town: Struik Publishers.

Spence, CF. 1963. *Mozambique: East African province of Portugal*. Cape Town: Howard Timmins.

St Mary's Cathedral. 1992. 'The Cathedral Chapel of St Mary on the Limpopo'. *The Parishioner*, March.

Tobias, P. 2005. *Into the Past: A memoir*. Johannesburg: Picador.

Van Riet, W. 1966. *Stroom af in my Kano: Avonture op Vyf Groot Riviere in Suider-Afrika*. Cape Town: Tafelberg.

Van Wyk, B & Van Wyk, P. 1997. *Field Guide to Trees of Southern Africa*. Cape Town: Struik Publishers.

Venter, S, Grosel, J & De Boer, B. 2006. *Greater Limpopo Birding Self-drive Routes*. 4th Edn. BirdlifeSA. Pamphlet/map.

Wadley, R. 2015. Geology notes. Personal communication.

Walker, C. 1982. *Twilight of the Giants*. Johannesburg: Sable Publishers.

Walker, C. 1992. *Dear Elephant Sir*. Johannesburg: Southern Book.

Warhurst, PR. 1962. *Anglo-Portuguese Relations in South-Central Africa, 1890–1900*. Royal Commonwealth Society Imperial Studies XXIII. London: Longman.

Wheatcroft, G. 1985. *The Randlords: South Africa's robber barons and the mines that forged a nation*. New York: Simon & Schuster.

Wheeler, Douglas L. 1968. Gungunyane the negotiator: a study in African diplomacy. *Journal of African History* 9: 583–602.

Wilson, A. 1979. *The Strange Ride of Rudyard Kipling: His life and works*. London: Granada.

Wongtschowski, BEH. 1990. *Between Woodbush and Wolkberg: Googoo Thompson's story*. 2nd Edn. Self-published.

Zeederberg, H. 1971. *Veld Express*. Cape Town: Howard Timmins.

Credits

Photographs

Allen, Dana: page 237

Barnett Collection: page 107 (left middle)

BSA Police Record Book, Tuli: page 99, 107 top right

Educational Wildlife Expeditions archives: pages 11, 37 (top), 45

Ledger, John: page 226

Muller, Pietman: pages 12/13, 41, 94/95, 104/105, 112/113, 122/123, 148, 151, 180/181

Norton, Di: page 16

Player, IC: page 69 (inset)

Rhodes, CJ: *Twilight of the Giants*: page 98

Spear, Carey Anne: page 31 (bottom)

The Bateleurs: page 59

Tiley-Nel, Sian, Mapungubwe Museum University of Pretoria: page 121 (both images)

19th century illustrations

From *Hunter's Life in South Africa*, 1986: pages 69, 76, 90

From *Portraits of the Game and Wild Animals of Southern Africa*, 1986: page 74

From *Twilight of the Giants*, 1982: page 92

From *Veld Express*, 1971: page 102

From *African Hunting and Adventure*, 1894: page 92

Maps

Peace Park Foundation: Craig Beech and staff are thanked for the three excellent maps on pages 19, 117 and 187.

Acknowledgements

The authors wish to acknowledge those who have given assistance, advice, wisdom and hospitality, as well as those who have given permission to quote or have provided photographic material. We sincerely apologise if anyone has been omitted. Work started in 2005 and much water has flowed down this river since then, and for us it has been an extraordinary journey. Thank you to those who have been so helpful in making it possible.

The publication of this work is due to the very kind sponsorship of Nicky and Strilli Oppenheimer and the Department of Research & Conservation at E Oppenheimer and Son.

We thank Duncan MacFadyen for the Foreword and Dr John Ledger for the Afterword. They are both tireless, committed conservationists.

Many people have helped us in so many ways and, in particular, we would like to thank: Warren Adams, Heidi Baer, Garth Barnes (WESSA), Pamela Barrett (BirdLife South Africa), The Bateleurs, Craig Beaton, Craig Beech and staff of the Peace Parks Foundation, Mark and Lesley Berry, Michael Brett, The late Colin Bristow, Glynis Brown, Vincent Carruthers, Sean Christie (M&G), Roger Collinson, Bridget Corrigan (EWT Source to Sea River Programme), Rob and Joy Cowan, Annemie de Klerk (LEDET), Paul Fairall (Jukskei River Forum), John and Wendy Farrant, Helena Fitchat, Andrew Gilfillan (information on the Anglo-Boer War – Tuli, North-Eastern Botswana), Judy Gournaris, Grant Hall (Mmamagwa), Christine Henselmans, Joseph Heymans, Peter Hitchins, Hector Magome, Mashatu Tented Camp (staff and guides), Marion Mengel (Friends of Nylsvlei), Pietman Muller, Sian Tiley Nel (Mapungubwe Museum), Nwanedi Resort (management), Mrs Joan Provis (information on 'Brownie' Ramke), Isaac Rambauli (Lake Funduzi and other sites), SANDF (assisted escort to the Madimbo Corridor), Dr Warwick Tarboton, Dr Sarah Venter, Richard Wadley (geology), Peter and Sean Waller, Anton Walker, Renning Walker and Wilderness Safaris (Pafuri Lodge).

Our publisher and staff are especially thanked for their commitment and dedication in ensuring this publication joins the ranks of important natural history publications, particularly Carol Broomhall, Kerrie Barlow, Megan Mance, Jenny Prangley and Shawn Paikin.

Finally, a very special word of thanks to our respective families who have encouraged us and tolerated our absence on numerous occasions over a number of years. Jill Bergman is especially thanked for her assistance to her brother, Peter Norton.